The ABCs of
Effective Feedback

· ·

Irwin M. Rubin, Ph.D.
Thomas J. Campbell, M.D.

· ·

The ABCs of Effective Feedback

Effective Feedback

A Guide for
Caring Professionals

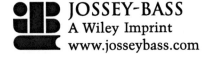

JOSSEY-BASS
A Wiley Imprint
www.josseybass.com

Published by Jossey-Bass
A Wiley Imprint
989 Market Street, San Francisco, CA 94103-1741   www.josseybass.com

Jossey-Bass books and products are available through most bookstores. To contact Jossey-Bass directly call our Customer Care Department within the U.S. at 800-956-7739, outside the U.S. at 317-572-3986 or fax 317-572-4002.

Jossey-Bass also publishes its books in a variety of electronic formats. Some content that appears in print may not be available in electronic books.

Library of Congress Cataloging-in-Publication Data
Rubin, Irwin M., [date]
    The ABCs of effective feedback : a guide for caring professionals
Irwin M. Rubin, Thomas J. Campbell. — 1st ed.
        p.   cm.
    Includes bibliographical references and index.
    ISBN 0-7879-1077-5
    1. Medical personnel—Rating of.   2. Feedback (Psychology)
I. Campbell, Thomas J. (Thomas Joseph), [date].   II. Title
RA971.35.R79   1997
610.69'6—dc21   97-14970
                                                                                  CIP

FIRST EDITION
HB Printing   10 9 8 7 6 5 4 3

Contents

· ·

Preface

. . . .

Without learning, we can't live. Without feedback, we can't learn. Learning is the key to individual and organizational excellence. Without feedback, learning from our experience is stymied. Without an effective feedback process, we are destined to fall short of fulfilling our greatest potential.

The field of health care, with its unyielding demands for increased productivity and accountability, is the backdrop for the book's vignettes and case study. The techniques and concepts presented in *The ABCs of Effective Feedback* will reward all caring professionals, and our work with clients in multiple sectors bears this out.

In this book, two tools are provided to enable readers to become both an effective giver and receiver of championship-level feedback. One is a map—a four-phase feedback model—of what needs to be done, and the other is a behavioral compass with pointers for how to do what needs to be done. We use the abbreviation *ABCs* when referring to the map to reflect the essential role played by an awareness of our behavior and its consequences in achieving win-win feedback. The integration of *what* and *how*—of map and compass—is an essential ingredient in the achievement of mutually growth-producing, win-win feedback exchanges.

The book begins with Chapter One, which makes the business case for an effective feedback process. Chapter Two describes both of the tools mentioned earlier: The Four-Phase Feedback Process and the ABCs Behavioral Compass Points. Wherever possible, we identify the specific points from our ABCs compass that are uniquely suited for each phase and the ways they can be used to help us chart a behavioral course for staying on a win-win path.

Chapters Three through Six cover each of the four phases in the model—Initiating, Formulating, Exchanging and Evaluating. Relevant behavioral compass points are identified to ensure that each of the four phases contributes to the win-win outcome being sought.

In Chapters Seven through Ten, we flesh out—and add heart and soul—to the underlying feedback structures. Chapters Seven and Eight focus on how the map and the compass fit the unique challenges of being a leader and dealing with interpersonal conflicts in a health care organization. What are the challenges of applying these models to people in positions of formal power? What might formal organizational performance appraisals look like if they were designed and conducted as a win-win arrangement? Chapter Nine offers four fundamental axioms—familiar truths reframed for a win-win feedback exchange. In Chapter Ten, we step outside of our conceptual outlook to reflect on the implications of two single individuals committing to using win-win feedback to improve their own relationship. Finally, the Appendix provides an example of the leading-edge feedback used by the players in the Chapter Eight case study.

Throughout the book, tips are provided that can serve as a checklist in planning for and learning from your many day-to-day feedback experiences. We use real-world examples and an occasional cartoon. In so doing, we hope to speak to both your left and right brains, to engage in thoughtful reflection from your hearts and your minds alike.

When it comes to living and learning, feedback is an essential ingredient. Improving the quality of our lives is one of the results of high-quality feedback.

August 1997   IRWIN M. RUBIN, PH.D.
                                       Honolulu, Hawaii

                                       THOMAS J. CAMPBELL, M.D.
                                       Dayton, Montana

To Douglas McGregor, a man who walked his talk.

I count as one of my many blessings the fact that I had the opportunity to know Douglas McGregor through more than just his pioneering writings in the field of human behavior in organizations. The clarity and leading-edge nature of his mind was—and remains—immediately obvious from landmark efforts, such as *The Human Side of Enterprise*. But no abstract medium could convey the more important message of the integrity and compassion in his heart. One story will suffice.

As a part of the Ph.D. requirements at Massachusetts Institute of Technology, all candidates had to pass an oral examination. This traditional rite of passage, conducted by the department's senior faculty, had the well-earned reputation of being the equivalent of an "intellectual hell week." Two hours before my own trial by fire, Doug came to me and announced that he intended to initiate a "minor" change in the process. The faculty grilling of the novitiate felt too much like a Theory X approach to Doug, a man whose life was built around Theory Y values. Instead, I was to "act like a professor" and give a group of students (the likes—mind you—of Warren Bennis, Edgar Schein, Donald Marquis, and other forefathers of the field) a brief lecture on my theory of human behavior in organizations.

While I do not recall any of the details of how I spent the next two hours (except that most of the time I was in the men's room!), I do remember very vividly the opening sixty seconds of my first formal lecture. After Doug announced the change in process (to the chagrin, I must say, of some staunch traditionalists), he simply turned to me with a smile and nodded nonverbally, "Go for it!"

I took a deep breath and thanked him, trying to sound as sincere as I could. In a painful statement of the obvious, I then admitted to a high degree of nervousness and anxiety. After managing to swallow back my raw fear for a second, I spit out the words: "So much of what I have to say, Doug, has been influenced by your thinking and writing that I'm afraid this lecture is going to sound very redundant. I apologize."

Doug then shifted his ever-present pipe to his left hand and rested his chin in the space between his right thumb and second finger, a trademark signal that he was about to deliver some thoughtful feedback with the "consummate skill and delicacy" he wrote about being essential to any and every "performance appraisal" situation.

To this day I can close my eyes and see the warm smile on his face and hear the love and compassion in his voice as he responded, "I hope you won't let my presence influence you, Irv, for I fully expect to learn something new today."

The ABCs of Effective Feedback is dedicated to Douglas McGregor and the integrity he lived and breathed.

—Irwin Rubin

Acknowledgments

. . . .

The roots of this book and its title, *The ABCs of Effective Feedback*, are grounded in experiences shared with others bringing the ABCs of win-win relationship skills to committed, concerned professionals across several cultures.

We offer deserved thanks to our valued ABCs colleagues Mary Bast, Bob Inguagiato, Nan Holmes, Kim Kanaga, Bev Kaye, Paddy Spruce, Frank Volpe, and Bill Walsh for giving us the benefit of their feedback. You are all released of responsibility for what we did with your valued input.

Sincere appreciation to Teresa Lever-Pollary, whose contribution includes an entire chapter, written on behalf of her colleagues at Nightime Pediatrics Clinic, on the role of feedback in creating a championship organization.

Heartfelt thanks for invaluable editorial support are extended to Wes Curry for his patience and persistence; to Tracey Bennett, who added her particular magic to the final draft; and to Jossey-Bass editor Andy Pasternack for his extraordinary sensitivity. Our hats also go off to Marcella Friel for her courage, understanding, flexibility, and competency in the hardest of jobs: being our final copyeditor.

We are grateful to Noreen Shiroma-Chun for providing her invaluable networking skills, which enabled us to meet various deadlines.

We believe the quality of this book is a reflection of individuals giving detailed, specific, honest feedback to one another. Many other people contributed to our efforts. Feedback is best provided face to face, and it is our intention to individually thank each of you for your special contribution.

A big *appreciate* to one and all.

I.M.R.
T.J.C.

About the Authors

. . . .

IRWIN M. RUBIN, PH.D., president of Temenos, Inc., brings his knowledge of human behavior in organizations to an international audience. Since 1966, Rubin has been involved in research and development efforts in public and private organizations in the United States and New Zealand. He received his M.S. degree (1963) and his Ph.D. degree (1966) in organizational psychology from the Sloan School of Management at the Massachusetts Institute of Technology. A coauthor of the standard university textbook *Organizational Behavior: An Experiential Approach*, Rubin is a former associate professor at Sloan School of Management, lecturer at Harvard Graduate School of Education, and codirector of the Health-Care Management Program at the Massachusetts Institute of Technology. He is an honorary member of the American College of Physician Executives.

THOMAS J. CAMPBELL, M.D., is a board-certified obstetrician and gynecologist. After receiving his M.D. degree (1960) from the University of Colorado Medical School he interned at King County Hospital and then completed a residency at the University of Washington. After sixteen years of clinical practice with the Western Montana Clinic, a combined group practice of over fifty physicians, he was selected to be its CEO and served in the position for seven years.

Having achieved his professional goals, Campbell now shares his experience as a group practice consultant. He also held two teaching fellowships at the University of Chicago and at Sydney University in Sydney, Australia. Campbell and his son, Tom, jointly own the only winery in the state of Montana. He is a fellow of the American College of Physician Executives.

The ABCs of
Effective Feedback

· ·

Making the Business Case

You may wonder how the topic of feedback, which Blanchard and Johnson (1982) suggested could be handled in one minute, can fill an entire book. In reality, the one minute of feedback that you might receive in a work setting could be the most important sixty seconds of your professional life. The messages that supervisors, colleagues, reports, and peers have to offer you can significantly shape your future. Consider a few cases where sixty seconds of poorly handled feedback led to a lifetime of debilitating consequences:

> The life of Charlotte Horowitz—whose dismissal [on the verge of graduation] from a Missouri medical school became a U.S. Supreme Court case—has become painfully public. . . . From all reports, she had an abrasive personal style . . . and interacted with the world like a fingernail on a blackboard . . . and she was brilliant. Everyone involved in the case could, at least, see that. Everyone's self-image is formed in some measure by the way that they are seen, the way they see themselves being seen. As their image deteriorates, their personality often shatters along with it. At that point, the rest of us smugly avoid them, stamping them "unacceptable" . . . because of their behavior. It happens all the time [Goodman, 1979, pp. 86–87].

Although Charlotte Horowitz ultimately might not have been able to curb her abrasive personal style and become a practicing physician, the absence of an effective feedback process guaranteed she never got the chance to find out.

Two other state rulings demonstrate the impact of poorly managed feedback processes. In the first case, Colorado's court held that an employee could collect worker's compensation for the stress-related consequences of a poorly performed performance appraisal. The fundamental issue was not the employee's performance but *the quality of the feedback process*. In the other case, a patient's malpractice suit named a host of San Antonio, Texas, physicians as accomplices. The plaintiff proved that the doctors knew their colleague's performance was impaired and never did anything about it. The doctors' failure to confront their colleague caused a patient irreparable damage—an unrepayable consequence compared to the $5 million awarded by the court (Schutte, 1990). While these cases may appear to be extreme, they show the impact of ordinary human dynamics that occur all the time in academia, corporations, associations, and all other places where professionals convene.

Fear of Feedback

Douglas McGregor, one of the great managerial thinkers of the century, points out that the very mention of performance appraisals creates an uneasy feeling. "Unless handled with consummate skill and delicacy, the feedback process constitutes something close to a violation of the integrity of the personality . . . leaving managers uncomfortably feeling as if they are 'playing God.' Yet . . . circumstances force us not only to make such judgments and to see them acted upon, but also to communicate them to those we have judged. Small wonder we resist!" (McGregor, 1972, p. 134).

What we resist persists. Our resistance must be overcome, or we will pay consequences like the ones we just read about. Without feedback skills, our ability to learn from and adapt to our experience is stymied. Continuous quality improvement, learning organizations, peer case reviews, and other managerial practices all stem from the same root: a desire to effectively give, receive, and utilize feedback.

Without experiential learning, progress and growth cease; individuals, organizations, and societies atrophy. Without feedback, we cannot fulfill our potential. We can ill afford to allow such a vital process to fill our hearts with fear at its mere mention.

Does this sound dramatic? Consider the following scenario. It's 5 o'clock Friday afternoon. Your supervisor's assistant delivers a memo asking you to be in her office at 8 o'clock Monday morning for a heart-to-heart discussion on your performance. If the message had come via voice mail, you would have been able to assess the tenor of the Monday morning meeting based on the intonation in your supervisor's voice; but reading between the lines of a memo gives you much less of a clue. Recurring mental conversations will take place: "I wonder what my boss has in mind," "What have I done wrong?" Sleep will not come easily. You won't be late, or rested, for this meeting.

The fear of feedback has primal roots. The first "performance appraisals" we received were conducted by our parents and teachers. A teacher's offhand negative remark about our first artistic effort likely triggered our tears and froze our creative juices. A parent pointing out how much better a sibling did on an exam crushed our budding motivation. It isn't necessarily what parents and teachers said; it's how they said it.

We find evidence of the power of early socialization experiences in children's stories. Let us take a moment and examine several passages from the familiar story of Bambi and Faline (Salten, 1928, pp. 174–181).

In his early "teenage" years, Bambi found himself in love with Faline. As they lovingly walked softly side by side through the forest, they were interrupted by nearby rustling sounds. It was Bambi's father.

The last time Bambi had seen the old stag—who was now ignoring him, while feasting on grass—was when Bambi was just learning to stand on his own feet. The gigantic gray shadow that spilled over their tanned coats drew an involuntary cry from Faline, while Bambi choked in fear. His need to protect his loved one was strong. He also felt excitement and admiration for his magnificent father. It was as if he was mystically viewing a replica of his own destiny.

Spurred by the silent tongue lashing he was giving himself for feeling so timid, Bambi announced, "It's perfectly absurd. I'm going straight over to tell him who I am."

Faline, sharing neither Bambi's courage nor his complex Oedipal needs, ran off crying and thus avoided the impending confrontation. Except for his pride, and the fact that the stag's eyes locked on his for a second before gazing haughtily off into space again, Bambi would gladly have followed her. Heart pounding, Bambi moved forward.

The next passage vividly depicts the authoritative early roots of our fears of feedback.

> Bambi did not know what to do. He had come with the firm intention of speaking to the stag. He wanted to say, "Good day, I am Bambi. May I ask to know your honorable name also?"
>
> Yes, it had all seemed very easy, but now it appeared that the affair was not so simple. What good were the best of intentions now? Bambi did not want to seem ill-bred as he would be if he went off without saying a word. But he did not want to seem forward either, as he would if he began the conversation.

One of the roots of failed feedback is planted in lessons we were taught about good behavior. Bambi, like many of us, was socialized to believe that it was impolite to initiate conversations with elders.

Respecting your elders meant speaking only when spoken to. On the other hand, Bambi was also taught that it would make others think he was "ill bred" if he walked by someone he recognized without an acknowledgment of their meeting. Such early implantation of double-bind learnings, as we shall see, can wreak havoc when it comes to feedback. Little wonder Bambi didn't know what to do. The consequences of feeling unable to act on our heartfelt intentions are further revealed in the fairy tale:

> The stag was wonderfully majestic. It delighted Bambi and made him feel humble. He tried in vain to arouse his courage and kept asking himself, "Why do I let him frighten me? Am I not as good as he is?" But it was no use. Bambi continued to be frightened and felt in his heart of hearts that he really was not as good as the old stag. Far from it. He felt wretched and had to use all his strength to keep himself steady.
>
> The old stag looked at him and thought, "He's so charming, so delicate, so poised, so elegant in his whole bearing. I must not stare at him, though. It really isn't the thing to do. Besides it might embarrass him." So he stared over Bambi's head into the empty air again.
>
> "What a haughty look," thought Bambi. "It's unbearable, the opinion such people have of themselves."
>
> The stag was thinking, "I'd like to talk to him, he looks so sympathetic. How stupid never to speak to people we don't know." He looked thoughtfully ahead of him.
>
> "I might as well be air," said Bambi to himself. "This fellow acts as though he were the only thing on the face of the earth."
>
> "What should I say to him?" the old stag was wondering. "I'm not used to talking. I'd say something stupid

and make myself look ridiculous . . . for he's undoubtedly clever."

Bambi pulled himself together and looked fixedly at the stag. "How splendid he is," he thought despairingly.

"Well some other time, perhaps," the stag decided and walked off, majestic but dissatisfied.

Bambi remained filled with bitterness.

Familiar rationalizations—"I'm not used to talking"; "I'd say something stupid and make myself look ridiculous"; "Besides it might embarrass him"—robbed the old stag of the joy of knowing, in the eyes of a loved one, "How splendid . . . and wonderfully majestic he is." The stag's own awareness of "how stupid [it is] to never speak to people we don't know" was not strong enough to overcome his pride. The absence of effective feedback, of a reflective mirror into his own soul, would leave the stag moving through his twilight years "majestic but dissatisfied."

For his part, Bambi would not only inherit the stag's majesty but many of the same unhealthy thoughts. If Bambi were fortunate, someone else might have the courage and skills to help him to see and accept his handsome, charming, delicate, poised, and elegant bearing. He'd need that boost to his self-esteem to heal his bitterness and assuage the feeling that, in his heart of hearts he was not really as good as the old stag.

Feedback Mania

Difficulties in giving feedback to and receiving feedback from authority figures are not confined to Bambi's world. Anyone experienced with corporate life will recognize similar problems. In an effort to meet the challenge, a feedback mania is sweeping the corporate world in the form of highly structured feedback processes, called 360-degree feedback, or 360s for short.

For those who are unfamiliar with the process, it works like this: a sample of people you've identified (and perhaps some your supervisor has identified) are asked to fill out questionnaires that solicit their perceptions of your leadership, teamwork, and communication attributes. Anonymity of the person giving the ratings is guaranteed. These data are often returned to a neutral third party who compiles and summarizes the data and prepares a feedback report for you. Often, however, does not mean always. As an article in the *Wall Street Journal* pointed out (Lancaster, 1996), some companies are using traditional 360s to determine who survives a reorganization. Having a subordinate pass judgment on a supervisor, according to the article, is "a little frightening and in the ordinary course of business, it's pretty easy to at least temporarily alienate someone."

Furthermore, unless you are the perfect professional, the results of any 360—anonymous or not—will be mixed. You will make certain discoveries: for example, 70 percent of those who responded feel your leadership skills are fine, while 45 percent of your colleagues feel your communication skills leave something to be desired. This feedback may leave you going around in circles, feeling good about how you lead and bad about how you communicate.

Unsigned, anonymous, summarized, averaged feedback on abstract attributes is of questionable value in improving the quality of relationships—in some instances, it may even make them worse. Why? Because abstract attributes are not to be confused with

DILBERT® reprinted by permission of United Feature Syndicate, Inc.

specific, observable, and quantifiable behaviors. If a specific negative behavior is not identified, an individual can't be held accountable for correcting or even exhibiting it, because she wasn't
provided the feedback she needed to correct her actions. If specific
positive behaviors are not identified, she doesn't even know which
specific behaviors to repeat to continue her positive attributes. Most
assuredly, she has no idea what to do differently to fine-tune her
communications. Unless someone actually believes she was trying,
consciously and knowingly, to be difficult, it is safe to assume that
she has been on her best behavior. Until she learns which specific
actions led respondents to say her leadership was fine or her communications were lacking, she does not know what her peers are
trying to say.

At the same time, asking for or providing face-to-face feedback
raises questions of how valuable the data will be. To illustrate the
point, consider this hypothetical situation: if a loved one of yours
were hit by a car while walking across the street, and the driver left
an unsigned note saying, "I did it, and I'm terribly sorry," how would
you feel? Anonymous feedback can hurt individuals and their relationships. Participants in the 360-degree process have reported
being subject to the third degree from a feedback recipient who was
certain they "knew" where the feedback came from!

Furthermore, 360-degree anonymous feedback can, ironically,
increase the likelihood that an individual behaves *inappropriately*
toward others. The only way for the 360 recipient to ensure that
she continues to work harmoniously with the anonymous 70 percent positive majority is to behave in exactly the same manner with
everyone, thereby possibly giving the equally anonymous less-than-
positive 30 percent cause to feel further misled. She might even
inadvertently leave the majority, previously happy with her communications, suddenly much less pleased.

Of course the worst consequence of the 360-degree procedure,
as it normally spins around, is that it gives neither the receiver nor
the giver of the feedback any practice in strengthening the face-to-

face, win-win relationship skills at the core of an effective feedback exchange process. Instead of reinforcing trust, 360-degree feedback, as it is typically handled, encourages people to go around in circles, telling third parties how they feel about first parties. This unhealthy and expensive lose-lose triangular game needs to end.

Reframing Feedback

If the medium is the message, the message of such 360-degree anonymous feedback is clear: direct, honest feedback, exchanged with compassion and sensitivity, is unhealthy. That message will breed lose-lose outcomes instead of win-win relationships.

In the chapters that follow, we the authors provide an alternative message. We uproot and reframe the negative assumptions and fears everyone carries about giving and receiving direct feedback. This journey requires us to touch upon subjects that may seem disparate and to examine and integrate two distinct but related lines of thought. One has to do with insights concerning the logical, left-brain mechanics of a structured feedback process. The other has to do with the right-brain realm of value-laden issues. The ultimate feedback challenge is to apply with consummate skill a mechanical model that demands the utmost delicacy. Consequently, a guide to feedback would be incomplete without some sense of common spiritual concerns, such as honesty, truth, and compassion.

Constructive feedback, like Wheaties®, is "the breakfast of champions." The implication of the slogan is that eating Wheaties makes one a winner. In truth, great athletes acquire greatness through commitment to the kind of improvement that only constant feedback of the highest quality can provide.

In our professions we also aspire to greatness. Winning teams, winning relationships, and winning organizations are made up of winning individuals. If we are to become the best we can become, effective feedback is a daily necessity. However, we can never lose sight of the fact, as McGregor said, that our intention is not to play

God. We need to see ourselves as others see us. Our intention as authors of this book is to empower all caring professionals to believe and accept that, as an anonymous sage once said, "If I could give you one thing, I would give you the ability to see yourself as others see you. Then you would realize what a special person you really are."

2

The Many Faces of Feedback

Feedback to a professional is like water to a fish: it's everywhere; it's essential; and it's taken for granted—until it fails. Two simple examples illustrate the point.

The thermostat in our room is a nonjudgmental, impersonal feedback device. When the temperature deviates from the level we set, the standard we have determined is right for us, the feedback mechanism takes action. It reads signals, compares them to the predetermined standard, and eliminates any variations. If our internal metabolism changes, or if the weather shifts abruptly, we reset the mechanism to better serve our needs. The feedback mechanism does not say what is too hot or too cold for us; it does not judge our experience. It simply reports the temperature status of the environment.

We have daily contact with mechanical feedback devices but think very little about the ways they work for our benefit or their parallels to our need for continuous interpersonal feedback so we can fine-tune our relationships.

A second example shows how much we take feedback for granted. Our bodies feel comfortable within a very narrow range of temperatures. They send us feedback signals when the temperature varies beyond this range to the slightest degree (even tenths of degrees). Sensations such as a shiver, a flush, or an outbreak of sweat alert us to take corrective action. If we ignore these warning signals, and conditions are carried to the extreme, we experience the consequences of hypothermia or hyperthermia, and we eventually lose consciousness.

Mechanisms such as internal and external temperature gauges, while being responsive to our needs, are impersonal in their judgments. By contrast, subjective emotions are at the heart of the feedback process in interpersonal relationships. The stimulus for a feedback exchange is a discrepancy between expectation and reality. A given situation could turn out better or worse than we expect: if it turns out better, we may offer some praise; if it turns out worse, we may offer constructive criticism. In either case, we compare what happened to our standard of how we think it should be.

Both machines and human bodies illustrate the dynamics of standard setting, measurement, and corrective action; in this way, they parallel the process between people. When we set the standard, the expectation of "goodness," we establish a particular value; a personal judgment between two people or two groups of people has been made. In other areas of our lives, one group sets the rules, and a second group enforces them. For example, the JCAH sends teams of evaluators into a hospital and grades "goodness" against a set of predetermined standards. Hospitals that fall below acceptable standards in an area are given lower grades and directed to improve before the next feedback visit.

Without question, we rely on effective feedback. Consequently, we need to view with suspicion efforts to objectify and depersonalize the feedback process. This is not to say that feedback data should not be measured as objectively as possible. But human bias is built in to any data assessment, so determining what is important to measure is itself a judgment call, a very subjective decision.

Setting Boundaries Around the Ubiquitous

Because feedback is an all-pervasive part of life, defining feedback in abstract terms gives us only part of the picture. "Two parts hydrogen and one part oxygen" defines the composition of water, but it doesn't convey the experience of drinking it or bathing in it. So let's put some stakes in the ground and attempt to define the ubiquitous feedback terrain.

The tenth edition of *Merriam-Webster's Collegiate Dictionary* defines *feedback* as "the return to the input of a part of the output of a machine, system, or process . . . that improve[s] performance . . . or provide[s] self-corrective action" (p. 427). Sounds simple enough. But feedback between humans raises the question, How does feedback differ from interpersonal communications in general? All interpersonal communications can be seen as attempts to influence others. One party's output is another's input, and vice versa. A silent "hello" waved to a friend across the street carries the unspoken expectation for feedback of a comparable form. A smile and a wave back constitute positive feedback, while a sour face constitutes negative feedback.

Because all interpersonal communications carry some element of feedback, and all feedback requires interpersonal communications, the experiences are interchangeable. Our purpose as authors is to broaden the understanding of and sensitivity to the oceans of feedback and communications in which professionals swim continuously.

Interpersonal feedback is by definition a process. And a *process,* our dictionary says, is a "natural phenomenon marked by gradual changes that lead toward a particular result" (p. 929). With that additional piece of information, our journey through the terrain of interpersonal feedback takes on clearer boundaries. Feedback is a dynamic natural phenomenon, and the particular result we seek is improved performance.

Our focus as authors of this book is to help you, our readers, gradually improve your performance and enrich your life through correcting your actions. We hope to show you how effective feedback can increase the occurrence of win-win, mutually growth-producing relationships. Where you choose to apply these learnings—for example, marriage, family, and work—are up to you. The choice of setting your thermostat and choosing how to use the feedback provided are your responsibility. Continuous Quality Improvement (CQI), a feedback-driven process, is not limited to teams and organizations. Experiential learning—CQI at the relationship level—protects us from the nasty consequences of accumulating emotional baggage (Rubin, 1991).

This point deserves emphasis. Counter to conventional thinking, the approach to feedback presented in this book will seldom be effective if it is used solely for the receiver's own good. The gift of seeing ourselves as others see us comes to us only when we take 100 percent responsibility for our half of every relationship. Win-win relationships don't happen by playing God; they happen because we imperfect human beings accept that progress, not perfection, is our lot in life.

Feedback processes that are not win-win by nature create unhealthy relationships that are not mutually growth-producing. Such relationships often atrophy and die. Giving and receiving feedback is an intimate human exchange.

The definitional stakes that we have placed on the terrain have brought us full circle from a comment made in Chapter One: "Without feedback, learning from our experience is stymied." We have not only the opportunity to use feedback and respond to our experiences by improving our behavior but also the responsibility to do so. The quality of our lives depends on feedback.

Traveling the Terrain: A Map and a Compass

Now that we've staked the terrain we intend to cover, we need to introduce two aids that will help us on this journey.

One aid refers to the four phases of an effective feedback process: Initiating, Formulating, Exchanging, and Evaluating (see Figure 2.1). This four-phase model will serve as our map, helping us to identify where we are and where we need to be headed. However, knowing where we are and where we need to go is only half the challenge; it's equally important to know which direction to move in and how best to navigate the terrain. The ABCs Behavioral Compass (Figure 2.2 and Exhibit 2.1) will be our second important aid. ABCs, as we mentioned briefly in the Preface, stands for an awareness of our behavior and its consequences. A variety of behavioral tools are needed to ensure that a relationship between two people becomes mutually supportive and growth-producing—a win-win relationship. Feedback ensures that all parties can become regularly aware of how their behavior affects the other parties and provides the basis for the continuous fine-tuning any dynamic relationship needs to stay on track. Unlike less-developed species, we human beings can consciously choose an alternative behavior when we become aware that a particular behavior produced an undesirable consequence. Therefore, the ABCs Behavioral Compass points the way to appropriate communication at each of the four points on the feedback map.

Herein lies one of the fundamental paradoxes of feedback: to improve the quality of my interpersonal communications (remembering that all interpersonal behavior is a form of communication), I need to use my interpersonal skills—the same skills I am currently lacking. The continued emphasis on the word *my* is meant to remind readers that each of us is responsible for our behaviors and reactions to others' behaviors and reactions.

In Figure 2.2, the points on the compass are graphically represented to parallel the four corners of the globe. The upper hemisphere contains the four *push* behavioral styles: *appreciate*, *describe*, *prescribe*, and *inspire*. Since *describe* and *prescribe* are factually oriented styles, they are positioned toward the relative "coolness" of the North Pole. *Appreciate* and *inspire*, consistent with their emotionally oriented natures, are positioned closer to the equator. The lower hemisphere contains the four *pull* behavioral styles: *attend*, *ask*, *understand*, and *empathize*.

Exhibit 2.1. Interpreting the ABCs Behavioral Compass Points.

In all interactions, human behaviors fall into one of two categories reflecting our use of *push* or *pull* energy. We use *push* energy when our primary objective is to have our thoughts and feelings better understood by another person. We use *pull* energy when our primary objective is to better understand another person's thoughts and feelings. Insensitivity to differences in energy modes can cause considerable interpersonal tension. We need to use appropriate *push* and *pull* energies to create a win-win relationship in which both parties understand and feel understood.

Push Communication Styles

When I *push*, I can

- *Describe* what has happened or what is happening
- *Prescribe* what should happen or must happen in the future
- *Appreciate* the significance of what has happened or is happening
- *Inspire* others to collaborate toward achieving common future goals

Describe and *prescribe* are both fact-based styles. When a giver describes, he uses data and logic to explain, debate, or justify a position or idea. When he makes proposals and suggestions for what will, should, or must happen in the future that rely on facts, data, and reasons, he is using his push energy to prescribe.

Appreciate and *inspire* are both feeling-based styles. When a giver provides direct feedback about how he feels about the receiver's past or current behavior or ideas, he is using his push energy to appreciate. When he uses his feelings to convince the receiver to join with him in achieving a future-oriented goal, he is using his push energy to inspire.

Pull Communication Styles

A receiver uses *pull* energy when she wants to better understand someone else's thoughts and feelings. When a person uses pull energy, that person may

- *Attend* to the other person by making herself receptive to what it is the other person is trying to push
- *Ask* questions that will help the other person express thoughts, feelings, or ideas
- Strive to *understand* the other person's message and to show that understanding through verbal and nonverbal cues
- *Empathize* with the other person's feelings

Attend is almost exclusively exhibited nonverbally. Put another way, people know we are not paying attention when we interrupt them frequently or fumble with papers while they are talking. Givers will feel sincerely pulled when receivers *ask* questions that demonstrate an unconditional open mind; they will feel deceptively pulled if receivers try to "lead the witness" by asking questions designed to pull the giver around to the receiver's position or to entrap them.

When a receiver demonstrates that she *understands*, she lets givers know she is paying attention to what they are saying and that she is listening with an open mind. Understanding, however, does not mean agreeing or disagreeing; it means simply acknowledging the giver's message. When the message involves how the giver feels about an issue or about himself or herself, the most powerful way for the receiver to acknowledge the message is to *empathize*.

Words, Music, and Dance

Effective use of the ABCs requires more than just an understanding of the words that differentiate a particular communication style. The music (our tone of voice) and the dance (our nonverbal body language) all become part of the message we send. Two issues are important in this regard.

1. Our effectiveness as communicators will be enhanced when our words, music, and dance are aligned. Mixed messages will occur when our words speak one truth, but our music and dance suggest alternative conclusions. Saying "That's a great idea" in a flat monotone while shaking our head vigorously "No way!" is an example of misaligned words, music, and dance.

2. When feedback is given or received, feelings are often aroused. In emotionally charged situations, most people put more credence in a person's music and dance than they do in the person's words. A flushed red face would be more believed than a string of verbal admonitions that "I'm not embarrassed in the least!"

Feedback can show us our blind spots in our own communication patterns.

Figure 2.1. Feedback: A Four-Phase Process.

Win-Win
Relationships

Phase Four: Evaluating

- **Reviewing "Sensory Activated Tapes"**
  (*These are mental conversations and scenes taped during previous interpersonal feedback encounters*). The receiver must reflect on the message received and its effect. This requires that the receiver attend to the words that have been spoken. Equally important will be the receiver's reactions to the giver's tone of voice–the music–and nonverbal body language–the dance. All three dimensions of feedback have the potential to trigger "sensory activated tapes."

- **Mutual Debriefing**
  Both parties have a responsibility to conduct one final mini-feedback process on the macro process they just experienced. They need to address the question, "How well did we do?"

Phase Three: Exchanging

- **Championship Challenge**
  The purpose of this phase is for givers to deliver the messages they have formulated while receivers work to understand (versus defend against) these messages.

Phase Two: Formulating

- **Turning Down the Tapes**
  The feedback process often triggers a host of old tapes relating to fears and assumptions about what is coming. The primary receiver needs to consciously quiet these tapes, moving them from the front of his or her mind to the background.

- **Preparing the Message**
  The primary giver thinks about statements that reflect the full range of his or her thoughts and feelings regarding the upcoming interaction and identifies statements that can be communicated both honestly and with compassion.

Phase One: Initiating

- **Timing**
  Are both the receiver and giver ready and willing to engage in all four phases at this time? The starting or finishing of major projects will often, for example, provide a natural transition point for taking stock of where the giver and the receiver have been and/or where they're going.

- **Negotiating Boundaries**
  Have the receiver and giver agreed on the boundaries of the areas of feedback? Do they agree on what will and will not be covered?

Figure 2.2. ABCs Behavioral Compass.

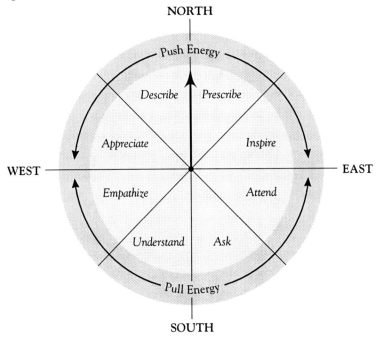

The Four-Phase Feedback Process:
The Map in Depth

The Four-Phase Feedback Process rests upon and flows from several key assumptions and values. For convenience, the two parties in the feedback process are referred to as the *receiver* and the *giver*. In any single interaction, one party will primarily be the receiver, and the other will be the giver. In certain sections of the text, fictitious names may be used in lieu of those terms. Within every feedback process—even those as brief as one-minute—there are vital micro-feedback cycles affecting the entire four-stage process. As a consequence of the shared responsibility for the quality of our relationships, and because of the give-and-take inherent in a win-win feedback process, giver and receiver roles change frequently.

Stage 1: Initiating

In the ideal Initiating stage, a potential receiver takes responsibility for asking for feedback. Such an action requires proper use of the ABCs (awareness, behavior, consequences) to ensure appropriate timing and clearly negotiated boundaries. This does not mean a potential giver always has to wait to be asked for feedback. A feedback process can be initiated either by a potential receiver asking or a potential giver offering. But before a giver offers it, he or she must determine the other person's readiness, willingness, ability, and interest in engaging in the feedback process—and then has to attend to the receiver's feedback!

Stage 2: Formulating

During the Formulating stage, the giver will determine—from a variety of factors, all of which reflect the giver's true feelings or thoughts—what to say and how to say it. Meanwhile, the receiver has an equally important, and silent, formulating task: shutting down the stream of internal dialogue, the tapes that get played in situations where feedback is about to flow. Skillfully applying the ABCs to that kind of self-talk will help receivers become more effective. (We address this challenge directly in Chapter Six.)

Stage 3: Exchanging

Both parties need the ability and flexibility to deliver the appropriate ABCs behavioral styles, as circumstances warrant, when the carefully formulated feedback is given. In addition to the guts of the matter, or the macrofeedback, many microfeedback events will occur in the exchange stage. The primary giver will periodically ask for feedback on how the feedback is going. Receivers will periodically be givers; they will prescribe ways the giver can self-correct to help ensure a smooth flow. In other words, while there is a formal exchange stage, the full feedback process contains many smaller exchanges.

Stage 4: Evaluating

A complete feedback process requires two levels of evaluating. One level takes place primarily within the hearts and minds of primary receivers as they evaluate what they've heard and what to do about it. A second level takes place between the two parties. If they have subscribed to our value of "progress, not perfection," each party will seek feedback from the other on how to be more effective in the feedback process.

The Compass: Tuning In

Having an ABCs compass is like having a schematic for your car radio. When you get some static, you have more corrective options than merely increasing the volume, randomly searching for an alternative station, turning the radio off, or giving the radio a whack. Each of these reactions has its counterpart in conversational static!

Awareness of behavioral options will not guarantee more successful consequences. Practice is needed to increase one's ability to put words into action. And indeed, it is more than just practice, because practice, rather than making perfect, merely makes permanent. It takes good practice to get good progress, and both rely on good feedback.

At the same time, a feedback process cannot be measured simply by whether the receiver changed position on the basis of what the giver said, or whether the receiver stopped doing what was bugging the giver or started doing what the giver suggested. The effectiveness of a feedback process depends on the two parties' abilities to engage in the process itself, on their feeling good about what was accomplished, and their feeling good about the part each played in the process.

Win-Win Feedback: Obstacles and Rewards

Change itself is a multifaceted process that begins with unfreezing, and unfreezing requires heat. We have all experienced defensive reactions to feedback in both their direct and disguised forms—from unspoken counterattacks such as "Who is she to tell me . . . ?" to the more self-righteous response, "Let he who has never sinned cast the first stone."

Even if we, as feedback receivers, have heard the things a giver says a thousand times before, hearing them creates strong feelings. Our behavioral habits—intimate and familiar parts of ourselves— are being subjected to the pain and embarrassment of a challenge. We react protectively, even if we've wished upon many occasions that this aspect of our character would vanish.

Between the heat of unfreezing and the internalization of refreezing of a new habit are the million-and-one convenient rationalizations that keep us from reconnecting to our birthright: the willingness, ability, and joy of learning something new. Feedback can help initiate positive change and make it permanent. But an effective feedback process is not about forcing change on anyone. Because change requires commitment and not just compliance, the decision to change is an "inside job."

Feedback offers receivers the opportunity to see themselves as truly special people, someone who the giver—an equally special human being—cares enough about to engage in this intimate exchange. In return, the giver will come away with more of the humility and grace required to be an effective receiver. For the giver, the gift is in the giving, whether or not the receiver ever does anything with the feedback gift that was given.

If, however, the receiver embraces the feedback and acts upon it, then the giver and the receiver will exchange more gifts of feedback, for two primary reasons. First, the setting of a new habit, like setting a new temperature on a thermostat, requires regular fine-tuning adjustments. Second, and more important, if two people expect to have a win-win relationship, they will experience the universal rule of reciprocity. Any attempt on one's part to create a permanent change in behavior will create the need for complementary changes in the other's behavior. The complementary nature of living and learning makes an effective feedback process a characteristic of all win-win relationships.

We don't expect individuals to put this much energy into each feedback situation. The detailed steps involved in regularly sinking fifteen-foot putts or consistently serving tennis aces boggle the mind. Analyzing them frame by frame, we wonder, Can I do that? It is unlikely that average recreational golfers or tennis players will spend hours reviewing tapes to improve their game.

On the other hand, life presents all of us with pregnant moments when we realize that what we say or do in sixty seconds' time could create a lifetime of consequences. It is precisely for those crucial moments that time spent learning the details of win-win feedback strategies could have big payoffs. We now explore those details.

. . . .

3

Initiating Feedback

The readiness is all.

—*William Shakespeare*, Hamlet

While most fans are settling into their seats at the sports stadium or the arena, the teams are performing initiation rituals. To determine which team will take the first shot, basketball games begin with a jump ball at center court. A flip of a coin on the fifty-yard line precedes the clock starting and can significantly affect the outcome of a football game. The winner of the toss gets the pigskin and the first opportunity to score; the loser considers wind direction and field conditions and decides which goal it will defend. Before Olympians go for the gold, they march in the opening ceremonies. Jai alai players file onto the court and raise their *cestas* to salute the crowd. Even before these rituals occur, all of the athletes have faithfully performed their own warmup rituals of stretching and flexing their muscles to minimize injury during the game.

Outside the sports arena, the world of human relationships has many rituals of initiation. From baptismals to confirmations to graduations, we acknowledge the transitions young people experience as they mature and grow. These initiating activities provide formal feedback to the world that the novitiates have arrived: a young male announces at his bar mitzvah, "Today I am a man!"

In the world of business, Americans expecting to negotiate successful deals in Asian countries must learn that a casual meal consumed over small talk is a required precursor to hard-nosed negotiations. To "talk turkey" while eating would be considered impolite and out of order.

The health care field also has its set of rituals. Surgeons spend at least three minutes thoroughly scrubbing their hands and arms up to the elbows despite the fact that their arms will soon be encased in sterile latex gloves.

However, most of us rush through a feedback exchange as if we were fleeing a burning house. The thought of "telling it like it is" drives us to "get it over with" as soon as possible. Thus the Initiating phase of the Four-Phase Feedback Process described in Chapter Two provides an opportunity for us to warm up and flex our behavioral muscles for the feedback event. Quite often this stage is handled poorly.

Short-Circuiting the Initiation Phase

Short-circuiting any natural phenomenon, any process, is bound to have consequences, and feedback is no different. A few examples will probably sound familiar.

> You and a colleague are rushing to get some data together for your mutual boss. Your colleague's habit of allowing all manner of interruptions when you're working together has always bothered you a lot. Guided by one of the rules of good feedback behavior taught by your parents, you've chosen to say nothing about it, since you have nothing positive to say. As the deadline looms on the horizon, and your colleague has taken yet another quickie phone call, you feel yourself shaking with frustration. Your segue could easily be any of the following variations on the "by-the-way" initiating style:
>
> "By the way, now that you're finally off the phone, I've been meaning to say something for a long time . . . "

"By the way, let me be perfectly frank . . . "

"By the way, I don't want you to take this personally but . . . "

While these statements will grab your colleague's attention, they will also pour gas on a fire. The fact that you've waited so long to tell your colleague how his behavior affects you is not his responsibility; it's yours.

In a similar vein, the warning that you are about to be "perfectly frank" is a good indicator that what follows may not turn out as "perfect" as desired. If you've been less than honest in your efforts to be frank before, this particular situation will be carrying added baggage. Unnecessary baggage, not feedback, becomes the straw that breaks the camel's back.

A typical variation on the "by-the-way" initiating modality is using the other person's agenda as a wedge to score a few of our own points: "By the way, as long as we're on the subject . . . " Imagine the situation just described, with the following variation: when your colleague finally gets off the phone, the first words out of his mouth are, "God, my spouse is always chewing my ear off about something or another. On and on, like a broken record, without a clue that I have other things to do!"

Only the most disciplined among us would resist the temptation to piggyback on such an opening and quip, "It takes one to know one!" However, sarcasm begets sarcasm. So when sarcastic feedback comes to mind—and it will—the best strategy is to bite our tongues.

In this situation you have one primary and immediate agenda: you need to focus your colleague's awareness on what the two of you have to accomplish before the deadline. The timing may not be right for initiating a feedback discussion about your colleague's behavior until you have cleaned out your feelings about not having had the discussion sooner.

You can use the ABCs Behavioral Compass to deal with the immediate situation. You might begin the discussion by describing the situation this way: "We've only got twenty minutes until D-day."

You could then follow with a prescription: "How about we ask your secretary to hold all calls for a while?" When the immediate crisis has passed, you could deal with the historical feedback issues. Raising them now, given the emotional pressure of the time deadlines, may only add to the crisis.

Now for a word about prescribing to people that they should not take our feedback personally. Just as many child-rearing books advise parents to address the child's behavior rather than attack the child as a person, it's important that feedback be framed in a way that does not leave the receiver feeling attacked. Saying "I'm concerned about the number of phone calls you're accepting when we have so much work to do" will not generate unnecessary heat by name calling. On the other hand, nothing could be more personal than a person's behavior, as the following true story points out.

> The CEO of a large nursing home chain called a special meeting to discuss the progress of a major project. While the specifics of the agenda were not communicated in advance, everyone knew the plug was about to be pulled on the project. The heat was definitely rising, particularly under the seat of the vice president of marketing, in whose area of accountability the project fell.
>
> To her credit, the CEO began the meeting by describing, in unemotional detail, the past and current financial performance—costs and benefits—of the project. She then turned to the vice president of marketing and, with obvious feeling, empathy, and sincerity, said, "Mary, I have some specific concerns about how your leadership of your group might have contributed to where we are at the moment. I hope you won't take my concerns personally."
>
> The pregnant silence that hung over the room seemed to last considerably longer than a moment. Mary, to her credit, took a deep breath, looked her boss right in the eyes, and responded with equal feeling and sincerity: "My leadership behavior is very much a reflection of my person. I hope you trust me and care about our

relationship enough to be honest with me. Otherwise, there is no way I can improve as a person."

No one said that feedback was going to be easy and that courage would not be needed! The courageous vice president in this anecdote was sensitive to the need for lowering the heat the givers were about to feel. Giving feedback to another person *should* make us squirm—to attempt to depersonalize an intimate human encounter seems to us to be exactly what is wrong with much of the feedback being exchanged these days. Many senior managers receive very heavy-duty feedback in the "don't-take-this-personally" style, as was the case with eighteen senior hospital executives, including the executive director, who arrived for work one morning ready to do their jobs of caring for people. They found security guards at their office doors and instructions to clean out their desks in fifteen minutes and then leave the grounds. Under the umbrella of efficient "downsizing," we are initiating feedback processes that cut people's self-esteem off at the knees . . . and that's very personal.

A Different Path

The ABCs Behavioral Compass can help feedback givers select a different path. Again, replaying the phone call scenario presented earlier: After your colleague complains about his spouse's insensitivity, try starting out by empathizing: "I'll bet it is frustrating." Then, follow by prescribing more effectively: "We've got a lot of things still to do ourselves. Let's put your phone on voice mail for a while." Remember, your immediate objective is to get the job done without further interruptions.

It is a very positive sign when a subordinate asks you for direct feedback. You want to make sure such a learning opportunity is not wasted. Careful management of the Initiating phase enables you not to get caught "shooting from the hip." Appreciate their asking you for feedback— "I'm really pleased to see you're so open to feedback"— and close with a *prescribe:* "In order to provide you with the most valuable information, I need to review your proposal first. Let's get together this afternoon at 4:30."

As the saying goes, "To everything there is a season, a time for every purpose under the sun." And timing is vital when the purpose involves "a time to seek . . . to speak . . . to heal . . . a time for peace." In order for the feedback process to work, both parties have to be able to fully attend to their own needs and be responsive to the needs of the other.

Other Tips

Internal circumstances—feelings you are carrying around about yourself—and external conditions all influence the appropriate timing for initiating a feedback discussion. The ABCs skill of attending will enable you to observe silently what's going on inside yourself, what's going on with the other person, and the circumstances you are both in at the moment. When in doubt, you can pull for help: ask the other person if now is a good time for the talk. And, finally, if you start, and it turns out to have been a mistake, return to *attend.* If the timing is not right, back off.

Avoid Carte Blanche Feedback

Only the most adventurous of us would ever consider walking into an unrecommended restaurant, waiving away the waiter's offer of a menu, and saying, "Just bring me the best seafood meal in the house." Yet many of us approach feedback in exactly this way. We approach a potentially delicate communication exchange with openers such as, "Whatta you think? How am I doin' these days?" or "Anything you want to tell me, just lay it on me!" Translated, these mean the same as, "I'm so hungry that I'll eat whatever you're serving up these days at whatever price you choose to charge."

This dysfunctional "carte blanche" approach is often evident when a person is fearful about initiating a feedback discussion.

Others use this style to say, "I don't really care what you have to say, but I'll ask to be polite."

Many people have bosses who are short on providing specific feedback but long on generalities such as"You're doing just fine." The parental golden rules they were taught might have included such "feedback truths" as, "Say nothing if you have nothing positive to say" or its counterpart, "No news is good news."

On the other hand, some of us may have been raised on not-so-healthy doses of feedback pablum such as "If I wanted you to know, I'd tell you myself" which has the corollary of "not speaking unless you are spoken to."

We can see the folly of the carte blanche approach by comparing it to a situation we all know well: the dynamics of buying and selling. Consider for the moment that a feedback exchange is akin to the interaction between a potential buyer (receiver) and a seller (giver). All experienced sellers know the power of making benefits statements—selling points that clearly link the buyer's explicit need to a feature of the seller's product or service.

Physicians follow this same principle when trying to convince a patient to have an operation. They know the patient needs to hear a "positive sales pitch": "You will have a 95 percent chance of surviving this surgery and getting back to a normal life." The flip side of the truth—"there is a 5 percent chance this operation will kill you"—is not a proposal that meets the "buyer's" needs.

After interminable imaginary conversations with your boss about how you feel you are lacking in feedback, you muster the courage to talk face-to-face. You walk into the open office, possibly blinded by your own anxiety to cues that the timing may not be right, and you pull up a chair. Very often, you sit in it with your arms straddled over the back, as though planning a quick escape.

The feedback process will be dramatically improved if both the receiver and the giver take responsibility to not allow a carte blanche exchange to occur. This involves using ABCs skills to put boundaries around what will be discussed during the interaction. It is our awareness that allows us to make conscious choices about how we behave and to adapt our behaviors to improve the win-win consequences. Your responses will depend on the specific circumstances you face. We are confident, however, that you will find the ABCs Behavioral Compass provides you with all the tools you need to negotiate clear boundaries during the Initiating stage.

We can prescribe some examples of things receivers might say and the points of the ABCs compass they cover in the Initiating phase to keep the conversation focused:

> "I've been thinking about my own tendency to . . . particularly when you and I are . . . [describe] I would like to change that pattern in the future. [prescribe] Do you have any suggestions?" [ask]

> "Three times this week you've told me I'm upsetting you. [describe] I can imagine how frustrating it must be to feel that I'm not responding. [empathize] Unless you can tell me more specifically what it is that I'm doing that is upsetting you, I don't know what to do to improve it." [prescribe]

> "In the past we've both dredged up a lot of old stuff in discussions like these. [describe] I apologize for my part in allowing that to happen. [appreciate] I need for us to stay current with the examples we use to make our points." [prescribe]

Follow the Compass, Not the Menu

If the receiver instead starts down the carte blanche path, givers don't have to follow. The ABCs compass provides tools to enable them to stay on track. Their primary objective will be to help set some boundaries. For example:

> "I'm really honored you'd trust me enough to seek my feedback. [appreciate] I don't find it works for me to shoot from the hip.

[*describe*] If you can tell me more specifically what you want me to focus on, I'll do my best to be helpful." [*prescribe*]

"It sounds as if you're concerned about where you stand with me. [*empathize*] Can you tell me what I've done or said that creates that feeling in you?" [*ask*]

If a giver feels the boundaries are not acceptable, and it is unlikely the result will be win-win, they will not hesitate to negotiate a more acceptable agreement. They can then determine what will and will not be discussed before proceeding:

"I suggest we split the discussion into two parts. [*prescribe*] The second area in which you've asked for my feedback sounds pretty emotionally charged to me. [*describe*] I'll sleep on it and get back to you tomorrow." [*prescribe*]

Prepare for the Main Event

Remember that part of the joy in any exchange of gifts is in the wrapping and unwrapping processes. So, first reconsider McGregor's warning that "unless handled with consummate skill and delicacy, [the feedback process] constitutes something dangerously close to a violation of the integrity of the personality" (McGregor, 1972, p. 134). All intimate human encounters go through a natural cycle of stages. The hit-and-run feedback style mentioned earlier will ultimately leave all concerned feeling cold and empty.

Second, the challenges of getting started don't have to be terribly complicated or time consuming. But ignoring important steps in the Initiating phase, in the interests of saving time, will invariably haunt you later. These preliminaries are most assuredly *not* a waste of time. Quite the opposite. Monica Seles does not deliver her cannonball serve without some preparation, without having stretched and flexed her muscles first. In the world of health care, there are numerous examples of analogous preliminary initiating procedures. A patient doesn't undergo elective surgery without having the procedure fully explained first. Furthermore, prior to the actual surgery, the part of the body being operated on would be shaved and scrubbed with an antiseptic solution while the surgeon mentally goes over the upcoming procedure. Nor does a surgeon expect to slice any half-moons in an unprepared patient. As Dr. Cameron Nezhat, an eminent surgeon at Stanford University has noted, "If someone scheduled for surgery tells me she's panicked that day and does not want to go through with it, I cancel the surgery. Every surgeon knows that people who are extremely scared do terribly at surgery" (Nezhat, 1995, p. 168). Getting to the heart of the matter in human behavior deserves comparable care and concern.

The ABCs behavioral muscles being limbered up and flexed during the Initiating phase are exactly the same muscles that will be essential during the main event, the Exchanging phase. If the microfeedback cycles in the Initiating phase are handled in a win-win manner, the prognosis for the success of the macrofeedback cycle will definitely be improved.

4

. . . .

Formulating Truths

Honesty without compassion and understanding
is not honest[y], but subtle hostility."
                    —Rose N. Franzblau, Touchstones

The formulating stage of the feedback process is an opportunity for both parties to prepare themselves for the upcoming exchange. For the giver, the challenge is to figure out what to say and how to say it; for the receiver, this task at hand is to turn down the mental tapes, the voices that urge them to take adversarial positions. (This challenge for the receiver will be explored in some depth in Chapter Six.)

The Formulating phase can be as brief as the space of a few deep breaths, or it can cover a longer period if a feedback agenda was set for later during the Initiating phase. As givers, we the authors have found that, unless we were caught off guard by a surprise request for feedback, the time allowed for the Formulating phase can be lengthy. Like many other people, we have found ourselves obsessing about how we can frame our feedback without sounding mean. The few pointers that follow will give some positive shape and form to this potentially anguishing process.

The Many Ingredients of Truth

Let us look at a sixty-second slice in time that offers a range of possibilities for affecting a relationship.

A health care human resources manager arrives home from work, bone weary from another Saturday spent managing the challenges of an intense reengineering effort to reduce inpatient capacity by three hundred beds. She's going home looking forward to a hot bath, a pizza, and a video movie—which would be like heaven. As she enters the kitchen, the first thing that catches her eye is a mountain of pots and pans on the counters. At the same instant as her nostrils sense an unfamiliar aroma, her husband's voice pipes up. With a mixture of enthusiasm and tiredness, he says, "Come and have a taste! My mother said it was terrific. She got the recipe from a friend."

She successfully navigates around the drippings on the floor, but the sleeve of her favorite cashmere sweater brushes a dirty utensil as she approaches the spoonful being held out to taste. As she swallows, her taste buds recoil.

"So what do you think?" her husband asks, stretching tired and pained back muscles. "Come on, be honest, the truth. . . . "

The *truth* is that there are multiple truths in any human interaction involving feedback. Our ABCs compass demonstrates a variety of ways to proceed, depending on the spin she wants to put on the situation. Each of several *partial* responses will reflect one truth in this pregnant moment. She could respond in several ways (again, the corresponding point of the ABCs compass follows in brackets):

"I can imagine this wasn't an easy recipe to prepare with everything else you had to do today." [*empathize*]

"Can you imagine how the subtle taste of the saffron could be enhanced next time by using fewer chili peppers?" [*inspire*]

"You couldn't have known that I had Mexican food for lunch and that it left a strong taste in my mouth. I'm not sure all of the spices you used got through to my taste buds." [*describe*]

"I'm wiped out, and I'm not sure I can give a meal like this a fair test tonight." [*describe*]

"How about we hold it until tomorrow and I'll try it again?" [*prescribe*]

"I can see how hard you've worked on this surprise!" [*empathize*]

"Thank you for being so willing to experiment. [*appreciate*] Your mother and I have different tastes." [*describe*]

"I wish I could say I loved it. [*describe*] But it isn't my cup of tea. [*appreciate*] Have you thought of inviting your parents to come and share it?" [*ask*]

These responses are not merely polite ways of avoiding the truth. They are labeled *partial truths* to emphasize the point that each of these statements could be reflective of truths in this situation, including the fact that the manager came home initially wanting to phone for a pizza.

If we put ourselves in the manager's place and, knowing what we know about ourselves—what we ate for lunch, how we react to being bone weary after working another weekend day, our reactions to seeing a mountain of pots and pans needing to be cleaned up when all we were dreaming about was a hot bath and a pizza—isn't it possible that we might indeed have a different reaction if we were to taste the food the next day? If the answer is "No way! Never!" then we cannot truthfully prescribe that suggestion.

If, to continue our example, the human resources manager is also an accomplished cook, and her palate can distinguish the subtle taste of saffron and the ways it can be muted by too many chili peppers, then she could, with integrity, inspire her husband to try the recipe again. This same truth from her personal experience and culinary skill allows her to be truthful when she describes, as part of her feedback, that she had Mexican food for lunch.

The key question to consider is, What are essential truths in a feedback situation? Just like the recipe, which had many different spices, the truth is made up of multiple ingredients. Identifying these and thinking about how to put them together can dramatically influence the taste your feedback leaves in your receiver's mouth.

The Benefits of Planning

Thinking through our options minimizes the possibility that we, if we were in the manager's shoes, would blurt out as feedback the two things we would be most likely to regret: "There goes your mother again, trying to poison me!" or "I love it, I really love it!" The former response could unleash a stream of feedback not likely to be win-win but very likely to make the downsizing alligators look like kitty cats! The latter response, while seemingly benign could have long-term negative consequences, as the following true story will attest.

Gail and her new husband, Fred, were invited to Aunt Sophie's house for Thanksgiving dinner so the family could get to know the new family member. In honor of the occasion, Aunt Sophie prepared a special version of the old family plum pudding. It was a painstaking process, using only the finest ingredients and the best of brandies.

At dessert time, with great fanfare, the flaming *pièce de rèsistance* was placed in front of the guest of honor. In spite of urging to "eat, eat," Fred served himself a tiny portion. He tasted the pudding and praised it to the roof. He then patted his overly stuffed belly, justifying his constraint (using the *describe* point on the compass). He then repeated for the umpteenth time, "I absolutely love the pudding!"

Until his death several decades later, Thanksgiving with the family had a familiar melodramatic quality. Aunt Sophie would phone weeks before the event to assure Fred that she'd be making his favorite special dessert again and, of course, to remind him that she didn't go through this painful, time-consuming ritual for just anybody! Indeed, she had taken to making two of them so he could have one to take home and enjoy throughout the holidays.

The ride to Aunt Sophie's house should have been filled with good cheer; instead, it was consumed with angst. The icy silence in the front seat was melted periodically with heated comments about the various prices Gail and Fred felt obligated to pay for being connected to the other's family. The children huddled in the back seat had to be extra good and not do anything to upset their father. They were to keep quiet and never to repeat anything that they heard their parents discussing, least of all their father's hatred for plum pudding!

This soap opera is familiar to all of us. We do not want to hear that our creations are not loved by those we would like to please. But feelings are a normal part of living, and negative *appreciates* can hurt. Our sensitivity to environmental feedback—to changes in temperature, for example—is delicate. If we weren't so sensitive, we wouldn't be human.

What Fred really wanted to say about the special pudding was, "I don't like it, and I wish you wouldn't make it for me again." But bending the truth is not the same as repackaging multiple truths in a way that makes them more palatable. Careful packaging, as Rose Franzblau's statement at the beginning of the chapter suggests, will increase the likelihood that our spoonfuls of honesty are spiced with compassion and understanding and not laced with hostility.

If concern for another person's feelings is not enough to induce us to identify the myriad truths of a situation and the best ways to package them, consider the following possibility. Many of us would treasure being able to increase our capacities to feel and express compassion and understanding for the significant others in our lives. Sowing these seeds of human kindness would reap more compassion and understanding in return. Whether or not the receiver accepts and embraces our feedback, carefully formulating it is bound to be a powerful win-win, growth-producing experience for us as givers. Our ability to experience compassion and understanding will be enhanced by our thoughtful attention to the Formulating phase.

Criteria for Packaging Truths

Not every truth needs to be fed back to the receiver. Having identified the multiple truths in a given situation, the giver must still decide which ones to include and in what order to serve them up.

The tips concerning timing that we provided in the Initiating phase are equally relevant in the Formulating phase. And while timing can be discussed abstractly, it is a skill that improves only with experience. The bottom line, then, is that, as givers, we must learn to do what any great chef does: season to taste. We have to prepare and package our feedback in a way that, according to our experience, leads us to feel confident that receivers are likely to experience it as a gift.

The reward for such careful preparation and packaging is a mutually self-fulfilling outcome; both giver and receiver feel like winners. The win-win quality of an effective feedback process reinforces itself as we learn to use all of our behavioral muscles. While we the authors can not be very prescriptive in the area of timing, we can offer a few rules of thumb that help prevent some pitfalls.

To begin with, givers must avoid the natural tendency to rely on the feedback-sandwich approach. The premise behind this frequently used approach is that tough pieces of critical feedback should be sandwiched between tender, positive ones.

If there are honest positive points among a giver's multiple truths that fit this situation, by all means they should be included in the feedback. But givers must be careful that the feedback provided fits within the boundaries that have been agreed upon during the Initiating phase for this interaction. And they must adhere to their own standard of truthfulness.

Here is an example of an *appreciate* that a receiver may well gag on: "I don't like this memo about patient waiting times, but I've been meaning to tell you how much I liked the way you arranged your office." If givers want their feedback to go down smoothly, the pieces—positive and negative—must fit together. To give an example: "I really appreciate your taking the time to try so complicated an approach to scheduling. I wish I felt differently, but I don't agree with your plan." This statement carries disappointing feedback at the end, but it starts with soothing balm to offset the sting.

If a giver is feeling anxious about how a receiver will hear some feedback he needs to deliver, he should consider the value of articulating his feelings up front. These are self-disclosed facts about our inner feelings about ourselves and fall into the ABCs category of *describe*. In contrast, feelings the giver has about the receiver, when they are shared directly with the receiver, are clear statements of the giver's personal standards, his judgments of what he appreciates about the receiver. When the giver describes to a receiver that "I'm feeling anxious about my ability to tell you how I feel without causing you undue pain or making you feel overly defensive," he is potentially doing several things.

In terms of the Initiating phase of the feedback process, he is setting the stage for the receiver to offer feedback. If, at some point in the macrofeedback exchange stage, the giver senses he's set the receiver off, he can initiate a microfeedback cycle. He can ask the receiver to tell him directly what effect his behavior is having on the receiver at the moment and thereby invite the receiver to be a momentary giver. In other words, the giver can ask for feedback if he suspects the receiver is not responding well.

By honestly exposing his humanity, the giver also makes himself vulnerable. Because the receiver is, in all likelihood, also feeling vulnerable in the Formulating phase, the giver's honesty can have a very positive empathic bonding effect. And the ability to *empathize*, as distinct from *sympathize*, is key to any win-win relationship, particularly when messages that reflect "the whole truth and nothing but the truth" are to be the medium of exchange. As Gretel Ehrlich sagely points out, "Honesty is stronger medicine than sympathy, which may console but often conceals" (*Touchstones*, Nov. 2).

Let's stay on this thorny issue of honesty for a moment longer. Think back over your own recent feedback interactions. Can you identify one where you know, in your heart of hearts, that you withheld feelings that were important for you to express? The words kept getting up to the tip of your tongue, but you swallowed them, perhaps with a forced smile on your face. You lost an opportunity to act with integrity, and your self-esteem paid a price that was small but accumulates over time.

When we leave an interaction knowing we have not spoken anywhere near the whole truth, we feel like a loser. And a win-win relationship begins with us feeling good about ourselves.

Comfort and Speed

We often don't have the time to get our feedback down to its most refined essence. Sometimes circumstances force us to meet a person's request for quick feedback. Under those circumstances, we would still strongly suggest that givers prescribe their boundaries before responding: "Give me a second to gather my thoughts."

At the same time, there are numerous circumstances where givers can and do invest time and energy determining how to approach a receiver with tactful feedback. If givers can discipline themselves to prepare more consciously for these pregnant moments, using some of the tips offered in this chapter, they will be approximating the kind of rigorous practice other champions engage in regularly. Just as important, such practice can help givers be better prepared to respond more appropriately in on-the-spot circumstances. Star athletes would never walk onto the playing field without first strenuously warming up all of their behavioral muscles. First, they talk themselves into the right frame of mind. Second, they mentally walk through anticipated crucial moments where the entire game might be on the line. The value of this formulating routine is confirmed in interviews with sports pros when, after a spectacular performance, they will commonly report that they were simply replaying mental videotapes.

As Douglas McGregor said, "We must take responsibility for judging the worth of a fellow man . . . not only to make such judgements and to see them acted upon, but also to communicate them to those we have judged" (McGregor, 1972, p. 134). Feedback is not a game. Telling other people honestly how we feel about them—or not telling them, as Dr. Charlotte Horowitz found out when she was dismissed from medical school in her final year—is anything but a game. To walk out on the field of play unprepared—as McGregor warns several times—"constitutes something dangerously close to a violation of integrity" for all the players involved.

Let us now turn to the Exchange phase and learn how to get our messages across in a win-win manner.

5

Exchanging Messages

I hear and I forget
I see and I remember
I do and I understand

—*Confucius*

During the Initiating phase, a receiver and a giver can agree on clearly negotiated boundaries that they seem to forget during the heat of their exchange. All of a sudden, the giver can find himself tempted by the carte blanche trap. His mind says, "As long as I'm at it, I might as well . . . "

It is vital that the giver formulate and see an image of the caring message he wants to deliver. Champions in all walks of life report that they visualize themselves succeeding before they act. When the exchange begins to heat up, this discipline will help givers remember the specific ABCs behavioral styles they formulated so that their feedback is truthful and compassionate.

However, while the Initiating and Formulating stages are vital, they should not be confused with the Exchanging phase. Only during an actual encounter do givers and receivers discover that none of their preparation entirely eliminates the feeling they get in the pit of their stomachs when they spot feedback ahead. This is a very important point: the anticipatory adrenalin flow is not something ever to eliminate. Sweaty palms and rumbling stomachs help us remember and understand something vital: that two imperfect human beings are doing the best they can. Preparation is essential, but it isn't until we as givers and receivers get into the thick of it that we really understand the consummate and delicate skill involved.

In the feedback process, there are no formulas for success. Consequently, this chapter is the first to articulate some of the most common pitfalls we the authors have witnessed—and experienced ourselves—that trip people up in the Exchanging phase. (While we use humor as a vehicle to make some of our points, we trust that readers already know that we do not see feedback as a laughing matter.)

After highlighting these typical pitfalls, we offer a simple mnemonic that we have found helpful. The bottom line, however, is that staying on course requires feedback givers to avoid typical misuses or overuses of the ABCs behavioral styles.

The Tyranny of Logic

Describing is, for many of us, an inherent style of communicating. Health care professionals, as a group, are educated, thoughtful people. In addition, many of us who work in health care and in other professions have beliefs and values that support the importance we place on being truthful and factual. We may have learned to see feelings as irrational or untrustworthy. Keeping cool is the key to success for those of us with overdeveloped *describe* skills.

Because of the emotional charge associated with feedback, we believe that concealing our feelings will make things go more smoothly. We use logic and facts to keep the interaction under control. While the ability to describe concrete examples of the situation is vital to an effective exchange, feelings are the essence of our being.

Logic also tyrannizes some givers' efforts to inspire. The strength of facts is their emotional dryness. Mixing them with emotive *inspires* waters down the message. Inspirational words and images come from the heart, not from our logical minds. This distinction suggests how the giving of feedback can become a win-win gift for the giver and the receiver alike. To deliver an inspiring piece of feedback, givers must be in touch with their feelings. A giver cannot inspire someone else if she does not feel enthusiasm and inspiration within herself. Being able to inspire a receiver with feedback, therefore, means that the giver must be able to inspire herself.

© News America Syndicate, 1986. Reprinted by permission of Johnny Hart and Creators Syndicate, Inc.

Facts Versus Feelings

Overreliance on descriptive facts can harm, not help, as the following example shows.

> Jack Martinez, medical director of a large HMO was repeatedly asked by both the nursing director and the head of clinic operations to do something about Donald Freeman, one of the director's physician colleagues, who also happened to be an old friend and a medical school classmate of Jack's. Dr. Freeman was exhibiting a defensive attitude and verbally abusive behavior that were upsetting the clinic staff.

Dr. Martinez began his exchange with Dr. Freeman by saying, "Don, several people have come to me and told me how unhappy they are with your attitude."

Dr. Freeman's response was, "It really bugs me when people talk behind my back! Who are they? Tell me who they are, and I'll set the record straight. Besides, you know how sensitive some of those women in the clinic can be."

Dr. Martinez saw an explosion coming and tried to deflect it with another unemotional, factual *describe:* "The problem was brought to me by people who trust me to keep a confidence. Who told me is irrelevant."

Dr. Martinez's refusal to disclose his sources provoked an even more vehement reaction in Dr. Freeman. "Irrelevant to you, but I have to work down there, Jack," he said. "Some friend you are, man. You don't even trust me enough to help me cover my flank."

© 1980 King Features Syndicate, Inc. World rights reserved. BEETLE BAILEY reprinted with special permission of King Features Syndicate.

Dr. Martinez's statement, "Several people have come to me and told me how unhappy they are with your attitude" clearly falls into the *describe* area. The medical director was acting like a reporter, describing the quantitative results of a poll of voter preferences, but it was an unsuccessful approach. Only firsthand descriptive facts and explanations are likely to work in this situation. In addition, Dr. Martinez inadvertently contributed to the triangle game, where one manager talks to another staffer about yet another's observations or feelings.

Behind this corrosive exchange was the misuse and overuse of descriptive facts. The sad part is that the feedback contained the seeds of several very important truths. Trust is not engendered by the triangle game. Many organizations are strangled by the amount of time and energy misspent by people delivering feedback to the wrong persons! It is the giver's responsibility to keep the feedback conversation focused and the accountability channels open.

Reporting Versus Describing

Reporting how others feel about a person's behavior is not the same thing as a giver directly expressing her feelings toward a receiver. Confusing *describing*—offering truths about how others feel about the receiver—and *appreciating*—the giver expressing her own truths about the receiver—will often cause a feedback exchange to blow up. Givers must be careful how and when they introduce thirdhand data in a feedback exchange. If and when third-party information is needed and appropriate, we urge givers to put very clear prescriptive boundaries around it beforehand. A quick return to a microinitiating session will enable givers to keep the Exchanging phase on track. Here's an example: "The data I'm about to give you as to 'who said what' is FYI only. I don't want to get sidetracked into a debate over it."

The Tyranny of Ambiguity

What do the following two statements have in common?

"I think that was a terrific report you wrote."

"I think the report you wrote was disappointing."

Both are pointing directly at the *appreciate* marker, a direct statement to the receiver of how the giver feels about the receiver's past or present actions. As stand-alone statements, both are also relatively useless in a win-win exchange, because they lack the specificity any receiver needs to learn from experience.

Moving Toward Understanding

The cheerleader approach to feedback soothes our egos, but it doesn't help receivers understand which specific behaviors they have to exhibit to earn another pat on the back. The self-righteous critic who stings our egos "for our own good" doesn't help either. "Honest criticism," Franklin P. Jones commented, "is hard to take, particularly from a relative, a friend, an acquaintance, or a stranger" (*Imagine*, 1995, p. 47). It is almost impossible to take if it does not include details. Receivers need to know both the pluses and minuses of their behavior, in detail.

The statements presented earlier would be much more helpful if they contained the following kinds of *appreciate*-oriented behavioral ingredients:

> "The two things I believe made your report particularly impressive were the breadth of your research summaries and the brevity of your conclusions."

> "The two things that most disappoint me about your report are the typos I found and the absence of any research support more current than five years earlier."

As any drill sergeant knows, there is a danger in overdoing detail. We've heard stories of people who proudly report that they secretly stockpile examples of a person's performance and accomplishments in their desk drawers to have for a performance appraisal. When receivers ask for more detail, they get inundated with constructive criticism–*appreciates* that have been stored for the occasion. As we see from the cartoon, this was certainly the case for our poor friend Beetle Bailey.

Appreciative Criticism

In Chapter Two, we stressed that some kinds of feedback are affectively neutral. The thermostat does not tell us the room is too hot or too cold; it merely monitors whether the temperature is what we decided it should be and acts accordingly. It compares "what is" with "what is expected" without judging our temperature setting as either good or bad. Through distorted perception and narrow use, we humans have, over time, taught ourselves to equate feedback with criticism. The same distortion and narrow use is true with the word *appreciate*.

The tenth edition of *Merriam-Webster's Collegiate Dictionary* offers these definitions for the word *appreciate*: "to grasp the nature, worth, quality or significance of; to value or admire highly; to judge with heightened perception or understanding; to recognize with gratitude" (p. 57).

Words such as *terrific* and *disappointing* are examples of one person's sense of the "worth, quality or significance of" something someone else has done or said. It is up to us as givers to learn to offer these value judgments with "heightened perception and understanding." In a win-win exchange, our intent is to be constructive with both our praises and our criticisms. This is why champions are so disciplined in their search for detailed feedback. It is gratifying for rushing guards to feel appreciated because they've sacked a quarterback, but it is more valuable, in terms of future performance, to have their coach point out exactly how they were able to avoid the defenders. A pat on the back is nice, but a pointer on how we earned the pat is even better.

The ultimate win-win value of a feedback exchange is contained in the last of the definitions of *appreciate*. To appreciate someone else's behavior is to recognize it with gratitude. What could ever lead us to equate giving constructive criticism with being appreciative, with struggling to "grasp the nature, worth, quality or significance with heightened perception and understanding" of something someone else has said or done? Carl Jung gave us the answer to this apparent paradox: "Everything that irritates us about others can lead us to an understanding of ourselves" (Jung, 1960, p. 516).

When a giver struggles to communicate something "constructively critical" about a receiver, the giver also struggles to accept that same (or a closely related) quality in himself. How else would he recognize it so clearly in the receiver if he hadn't been familiar with it in himself? When givers learn to see and offer constructive *appreciates* with such humility, they have an opportunity to recognize—and gratefully learn from—a truth about themselves and about all of us: at the core, we are all imperfect human beings struggling to live our lives gracefully.

One final warning about giving *appreciates* before we turn to potential pitfalls with ambiguous *prescribes*. At some point in a feedback exchange, a receiver and/or a giver may find it necessary to apologize for a mistake. We see apologies as attempts to appreciate, a kind of shorthand "thanks" for the other person's tolerance. If we allow ourselves to repeat Nancy's misdirected use of an appreciative apology, we might end up getting slugged.

Be Careful What You Prescribe

There is a spiritual axiom that cautions us to be very careful what we ask for because we might get it. The same caution applies to the

NANCY® reprinted by permission of United Feature Syndicate, Inc.

prescribe point on our behavioral compass. A feedback exchange will probably include multiple opportunities for givers to suggest future actions that would maintain the receiver's current *appreciates* and/or provide givers the opportunity to offer some new ones.

Sometimes, therefore, the most powerful prescribe statement we can make is to tell a person to "Keep it up!" Ken Blanchard challenged us to catch someone doing something well (Blanchard and Johnson, 1982). When you catch them, be careful and specific about what you prescribe. Don't just use the word *it*. If you are the receiver of such an ambiguous directive, you may want to enjoy the moment, appreciate the giver's behavior, say, "Thanks for the feedback," and then ask for details: "Can you give me a specific example of what's worth repeating?"

Framing

It is also important for givers to frame their *prescribes* in the first person singular, to say *I* not *we*. Such framing avoids two traps. The first trap is believing that by introducing the word *we* you induce others to bend under the weight of the number of people who support your view. To suggest that "we would like to see more detailed research in your subsequent reports" may be true, but it is not an effective *prescribe*. It's a *describe*. The second trap is using the *describe* style at all when what is called for is *prescribe*. There is nothing inherently wrong with objective data, but there is a different quality of communication that occurs when a giver looks a receiver in the eye and makes an *I* statement that expresses her own needs and expectations and sets her own standards.

Mutual Commitment

We need to address the fundamental fact that feedback is an opportunity for us to change our behavior. Feedback is a gift to a receiver, not a dose of medicine to be forced down the receiver's throat. Furthermore, it is meant to be a win-win, growth-producing interaction. At some point, a giver may need to offer a specific *prescribe*, one that promises mutual benefit. It is really two directives, two pre-scribes—one that the giver needs the receiver to commit to do and one the giver must commit to doing on her own behalf. "If you'll commit to telling me specifically how I can improve, I'll work on being more attentive when I disagree with you." This "contract" creates the basis for a long-term win-win relationship.

Threats

Sometimes, despite our idealism, when we are receivers we find our-selves in feedback sessions that degenerate into thinly veiled threats ("Do it or else!"). At this point, it is important to recognize that we, as receivers of such feedback, always have a choice. Formal employ-ment contracts can succeed only in getting our bodies to show up to work. They cannot force us to use our minds to their fullest potential. Only a win-win exchange can really get us to "do it"—with no "or else" on the other end of the line.

Resolving "do-it-or-else" situations rests upon the outcome of the cost-benefit analyses we do in our heads. The bottom-line ques-tion is always the same: "How much of my self-esteem is it worth to stay in a situation given the exchange rate—feedback—being offered to me in return?" If the answer is "too much," we conclude that the return on the investment is bad business. We get a divorce. We quit our job. We take steps to seek a better investment. In the business of living, we are all CEOs who call the shots.

These are bottom-line "points of no return." No matter what the bottom-line decision turns out to be—to stay or to go—the rela-tionship with a spouse, an employer, or a lifestyle choice will never be the same. An ultimatum is an either/or *prescribe* with no latitude, no room to negotiate—"If you don't . . . I'm going to . . .!" Such *pre-scribes* ought to be used sparingly, if at all, and considerable time should be spent in the Formulating phase to identify all the poten-tial consequences of such a communication style.

The Value of Pacing

In Chapter Two we looked at the *push* and *pull* styles of communication. *Pull* feedback—trying to understand others' needs—requires a comparable level of "consummate and delicate" skill to create win-win feedback exchanges. At a minimum, as givers we must continue to attend to the concerns of receivers and to the impact our feedback is having on them. Like a skilled marshall arts expert, we must stay attuned to receivers in order to pace the feedback exchange and not throw them off balance. Pacing is to the human process of feedback what a servomechanism is to the functioning of a piece of machinery. As givers, we must remain sensitive to how much feedback receivers can absorb and process. It makes no sense to keep pouring water onto a plant when it is spilling over the top of the pot. Yet this is exactly what many givers do with feedback when either the giver or the receiver is rushing or feeling anxious about the exchange. We need to stop for a second and allow the message to permeate deeply.

Simply sitting with mouth shut is not all there is to an *attend*. Many of us are skilled at being physically present but are often miles away in our minds and hearts. The real challenge is turning down the mental tapes, the ever-present critics. In order to understand and empathize, we have to be fully in touch with receivers. We must sincerely get the information, facts, and feelings. Only then will we be able to read the music in the receiver's tone of voice and the dance in the body language. What we don't listen to we can't understand. To walk in the other person's shoes, we must feel what they are feeling. "For better or worse," *attend* is the gateway style to the remaining *pull* tools.

FOR BETTER OR FOR WORSE © 1988 by Lynn Johnston Prod., Inc. Reprinted with permission of UNIVERSAL PRESS SYNDICATE. All rights reserved.

The *Ask* Direction

The ability to turn our behavioral compass quickly and appropriately toward the *ask* direction can make or break the Exchanging phase. Whenever I as a giver am uncertain about how I am coming across or what to do next, I can ask you, the receiver, for feedback. This is an essential example of a microfeedback cycle within the macrofeedback cycle.

Asking open-ended, nonleading questions can be challenging. Sometimes our *push* muscles are so overdeveloped that, even when we try to *pull*, our attempts to seek input become closed-ended, leading, and therefore rhetorical. They are really directive statements, *prescribes* hidden behind a question mark.

A Helpful Mnemonic

We refer to the techniques that help to minimize emotional blowups as the D.A.P. cycle. It consists of three parts:

1. *Describe* your observation of what has happened in the past or is happening at the moment.

2. *Appreciate* the significance or value, to you personally, of what you have just described.

3. *Prescribe* your suggestions and proposals for what could, should, or needs to happen in the future.

Very importantly, all of the D.A.P. points should fit within the agenda that givers and receivers negotiated during the Initiating phase. If it is a part of the larger agenda, then it is a scenario that givers have mentally rehearsed during the Formulating phase so that, during the Exchanging phase, they are simply replaying the video of their success.

To be absolutely certain the message has been received, even if it has not necessarily been accepted or agreed to, givers should add a final, small *prescribe:* "I need you to paraphrase what I've just said so I can be certain I've been clear" or "Please summarize what you've heard me say so I can check my own clarity." Doing this one last step will minimize the number of feedback messages that givers thought were delivered but that never got through to receivers because they tuned out during the transmission. This is very likely to happen, for example, if any of the giver's behaviors could upset the receiver.

Our D.A.P. mnemonic is familiar. Physicians frequently employ it when giving patients feedback. They often begin with a *describe* of the test results: "The laboratory results and angiogram confirm our diagnosis of a possible heart problem." Physicians who are more patient-oriented may add some *appreciates*: "I am pleased to see your weight coming down, and I'm disappointed that, despite my previous warnings, you continue to smoke." Of course, they close with a punch line *prescribe*: "I need you to sign up for our stop-smoking classes immediately." And the very best of them, as mounting research confirms (Levinson and others, 1997), include the final, small *prescribe*: "Now, would you please summarize what you've heard me say to you?" Those who skip this final point often end up with a noncomplying patient who returns for additional expensive care.

Building Appreciation

When an *appreciate* requires both praise and criticism, as in the example just presented, givers need to be very careful about connecting the two. Many of us have a habit of using words such as *however* or its more depreciating counterpart *but*. Both discount the positive affect offered by the praise. By contrast, the word *and* is more likely to be received positively.

Let's revisit the example presented earlier about the report and the tyranny of ambiguity and see how a complete D.A.P. might look in that case:

> *Describe:* "I notice that your report covered all the topics we discussed and that your conclusions were half the length of your last report's. The bibliography had no references after 1990, and there were six typos."

> *Appreciate:* "The two things that I believe made your report particularly impressive are the breadth of your research summaries

and the brevity of your conclusions. And the two things that most disappoint me about your report are the typos I found and the absence of any research support more current than 1990."

Prescribe: "Next time, I'd like you to be sure and use your spell check. If you need time to go to the main library to get more current references, just let me know, and I'll make sure your desk is covered."

While these are admittedly a lot of words to put together, the giver didn't have to rely on thinking up all of them on the spot. This is the benefit of the Formulating phase: givers can do the hard and important thinking in advance, which provides support for any feedback they might need to offer.

Win-Win Confrontation

Merriam-Webster's Collegiate Dictionary defines *confront* as "to face, especially in a challenge; to meet face to face." We're afraid that if we confront, we will no longer be liked. This natural concern leads us to another paradox. If, as givers of feedback, we withhold our true feelings about the receivers, what has been gained? The receiver has been robbed of the gift of seeing herself as others see her. Whatever feelings receivers have about givers as a result—"Always so nice! So complimentary! Such a dear friend!"—are, in fact, distortions. As givers we also rob ourselves of the gift of having receivers see us honestly. Instead of initiating a win-win exchange, we're brewing the ingredients of a lose-lose bad deal. Hugh Prather captured it well when he said, "Some people will like me and some won't. So I might as well be myself, and then at least I'll know that the people who like me, like me" (*Imagine,* 1995, p. 19).

The Bambis of our world give us yet another perspective. Animals will regularly confront one another and "knock heads" in their style of feedback exchanges. A value of this instinctive ritual is for them to help each other "sharpen their points" so that, when there is a need to defend against a real enemy, they are ready. The unspoken, inbred boundary rule guiding these win-win confrontations is quite simple: either party can call a halt without losing face, and neither will push so hard as to inflict permanent damage on the other. Our simple D.A.P. mnemonic is meant to allow us to exercise the same care and concern.

Douglas McGregor warned us, "circumstances [will] force us to make such judgements and to see them acted upon, but also to communicate them to those we have judged" (McGregor, 1972, p. 134). So the next time you feel the urge to zap someone, pause for a moment, think about the truths you might be able to exchange, and D.A.P. them instead!

6

. . . .

Evaluating the Feedback Process
and Outcomes

When an intense Exchange phase has come to a close, givers and receivers alike may breathe a sigh of relief—but not the feedback champions! If they're not immediately replaying in their mind the last ace at match point, they will be glued to the video replay the next morning—whether they won or lost. A feedback exchange not guided by win-win intentions can easily turn into a lose-lose battle. One person walks away silently smug: "I sure told her off!" The other person silently promises, "I'll get even next time!" A lion's share of learning from the feedback process can come from the "post-game" evaluation.

The Evaluating phase takes place at two levels. Let's look at those levels in turn.

Level One: What Happened Between Us?

The first level requires the two parties to take a few additional minutes to review the quality of their interaction. If time does not permit this level of evaluating to be accomplished together, each party may still find it valuable to ponder how well they have met the criteria for championship feedback.

To determine this, participants can use a checklist such as the one shown in Exhibit 6.1, which summarizes our normative prescriptions for feedback between two people. Take a moment to review it.

Exhibit 6.1. "Championship Feedback": Key Ingredients.

For givers and receivers to consider together:

A. What, When, and Where
   - Were the time and place appropriate for the feedback exchange?
   - Did we clearly agree on the agenda?
   - How realistic was the agenda?
   - How current and recent were the events we agreed to discuss?

B. How
   - Did we use relevant descriptive facts unemotionally?
   - Did we provide detailed *appreciates* and, wherever possible, balancing praise and constructive criticism?
   - Did we deliver constructive criticism compassionately?
   - Did we provide crystal clear, unambiguous *prescribes*?
   - Did we offer mutually beneficial exchanges?
   - Did we D.A.P. (*describe, appreciate, prescribe*) each other instead of zap each other?
   - Did we attend each other patiently and nondefensively without interruption?
   - Did we ask open-ended, nonjudgmental, nonleading questions?
   - Did we demonstrate understanding verbally and nonverbally?
   - Did we acknowledge and accept each other's feelings empathetically?

C. Effect and Affect
   - Did we schedule a follow-up time to explore important unfinished issues?
   - Did we take responsibility to implement the feedback we received?
   - Can we both answer yes to the following questions:
     - Do I feel really good about what we accomplished?
     - Do I feel really good about how I conducted myself?
     - Do I feel really good about how you conducted yourself?

If both participants can answer yes to the last three questions in the exhibit, then a win-win exchange did indeed occur, and congratulations are in order.

Reviewing the Exchange

The four questions under "what, when, and where" all have to do with the Initiating phase. Although an agenda was clearly agreed upon at the outset, participants might discover that the feedback turned out to be more than they imagined. The dynamic nature of two people interacting face-to-face (versus, for example, the sending of a letter or e-mail) often results in a feedback exchange taking longer than planned. Feedback is sometimes easier to take in smaller doses.

Currency of events addressed by feedback is important. As a general rule, *appreciates* (the A. of D.A.P.) are more effective when they are delivered close to the time of the behavior being described (the D.). By contrast, old feedback has two lose-lose consequences. First, by withholding or delaying constructive criticism, the eventual giver is responsible for extending the situation. Like Charlotte Horowitz, the abrasive but brilliant medical student we met in Chapter One, the person who needs the feedback may continue to suffer the "agony of defeat" without knowing she is losing and why—until it's too late. Second, by delaying or withholding hard-earned praise, the giver robs the receiver of the joy of victory.

The ten questions under the "how" portion of the checklist all refer to the use of the ABCs Behavioral Compass. Consider the question "Did we deliver constructive criticism compassionately?" In the situation of an employee being let go from work, meeting this criteria is extremely demanding. Extraordinary compassion and skill in the use of the ABCs compass will be necessary to deliver the final *prescribe* in a D.A.P.—"You will have to seek a job elsewhere"— while not coming across sounding negative or cruel. (Dynamically, this is no different than a physician telling a patient that he or she is terminally ill.) Win-win may seem impossible under these circumstances, and it probably is—in the short run. On the other hand, a senior manager reported having the following experience when he had to give his people feedback on available severance and downsizing options after a merger with another hospital. His CEO encouraged him to do some careful planning prior to dealing with this emotionally charged issue. So he spent considerable time formulating all the truths, not just the bottom line of needing to reduce the size of his staff. He even spent time imagining how the receiver might feel so he could have some sense of empathy. His results, summarized as follows, illustrate that even the most devastating events, if handled with dignity and compassion, are manageable: "Eight were area managers, and one was a manager at the same level as I. It wasn't easy, but I used my ABCs feedback skills and felt that company objectives were met and that people were satisfied with the explanations and procedures used. They left the company with dignity and no ill feeling. One even wrote a note thanking me for the way I handled the situation!" (Rubin, 1991). While we do not know the exact words used in this feedback exchange, we do know the person spent time replaying the interaction in his own mind and asking others for feedback as to how they felt about the way he handled the situation. It is also clear that, whatever specific ABCs styles he used, they must have been exemplary of win-win for a person being let go of their job to send a thank you note to the person delivering the bad news. More common are newspaper accounts of angry employees exacting revenge for the way their terminations were handled. Individuals who leave a job with their dignity and self-esteem intact don't bomb the office they left.

Ofttimes, we can only hope to soothe the shock and rage of someone who has been fired. Givers hope not to make the situation worse by handling it inhumanely. To be told not to take it personally is not an act of empathy. James Autry puts it succinctly: " . . . [because] nothing [is] as demanding of nerve, as gut wrenching, or as emotionally debilitating [to both parties] . . . there's just one way to fire someone: with love and support and deep, deep regret" (Autry, 1991, pp. 112–113).

The Closing Evaluation

Participants' long-term learning will be enhanced when they conduct one more shorter D.A.P. cycle. Using Exhibit 6.1, they would exchange feedback on their perceptions and experiences of each other as receivers and givers during the preceding interaction. This might result in a closing evaluating D.A.P. such as this one:

> *Describe:* "You said you wanted to focus this feedback discussion on the blowup we had last week. Your specific goal was to not get defensive when I told you things you disagreed with."

> *Appreciate:* "I was really impressed with your ability to 'take a deep breath' before reacting to my feedback. I was also grateful you were able to catch yourself starting to expand our agenda to points outside last week's blowup."

> *Prescribe:* "Please keep being so attentive and self-disciplined. And if I could have done anything during our discussion to help you stay focused even more, I need you to tell me."

When participants identify both shortfalls and potential improvements, they benefit from the Evaluating phase by learning from mistakes, not assigning blame. They review the process, not the content, of the feedback.

If participants don't have a lot of time, they may consider this option. Each participant takes thirty seconds to read silently over the checklist and formulate one final D.A.P. to exchange:

- *Describe* what sticks out in each of your minds about what just transpired.

- *Appreciate* what each of you has described, and tell the other about it.

- *Prescribe* one thing that each could do that would improve a good effort even more.

If none of the above is feasible, even simply reviewing and contemplating the checklist will raise the participants' awareness.

Level Two: What Happened Within Us?

The second challenge in the Evaluating phase is more demanding, taking place at an individual, personal level. Both receivers and givers could learn a lot about themselves from the following introspective process. The examples are not taken from the professional world, but from the world of home and family.

A man cooked a soup from a new but bold recipe. Drawn by the aromas wafting from the kitchen, his spouse walked in and asked for a taste. Somewhat hesitantly, he passed a spoonful over, imagining the final verdict. His internal feedback included a host of negative *appreciates* and stern *prescribes*: "You shouldn't have wasted your time spending all day on one soup," "I told you to stick with what works," and "You know I don't like spicy stuff." This anticipation of feedback triggered a series of mental tapes laden with worry.

We've all known people who are quick on the defensive trigger. (Indeed, we've shot down a few unsuspecting messengers ourselves!) The feedback playing in their heads has two potential lose-lose consequences. One consequence is that, because of the reduced ability to attend to what is being said (because they're distracted by what they expect to be said, by what is being said in their mind), they run the risk of not hearing everything that's said. Have you ever heard someone totally miss a word of praise or react to it with a look that says, "Yeah, and what do you want from me?" You can be certain that the person believes that the best defense against getting bruised is to be offensive first.

The second predictable consequence could be more painful than missing out on the nurturing power of hard-earned praise. Unless the receiver of off-putting defensiveness is very careful, she might resent being misheard and misjudged. If those feelings are allowed to fester, the person ends up being the giver of exactly what is expected: verbal or nonverbal "constructive criticism" without a whole lot of compassion. Chalk up another self-fulfilling—actually self-unfulfulling—prophecy driven by unexamined self-talk.

Let's return to the kitchen. After a few moments the chatter going on in the cook's head faded, and he breathed a sigh of relief as he saw a broad smile come across his spouse's face. The words *delicious* and *fabulous* echoed in his ears as he turned back to his creation.

Shortly after the positive feedback sank in, a new round of self-talk began, snippets of old conversations he had a long time ago. "Boy was that a stroke of beginners luck, don't let it go to your head." "You may be able to cook, but what about the five thumbs you've got when it comes to carpentry?" "Too bad you're not as good a writer as a cook!" "Remember who it was who taught you in the first place!" How long would we listen to someone else if they spoke to us in this manner?

In the same way win-win feedback can be a gift to others, the feedback we give ourselves can also be a gift. Although we may engage in self-talk continually, it is often loudest when we are anticipating or engaging in a feedback exchange. Feedback from others can remind us of times gone by when significant people forced feedback on us. Our minds become echo chambers. Messages from the outside trigger sensory-activated tapes (S.A.T.s) stored in our minds. S.A.T.s drown out or distort the feedback being received. Such self-talk blocks accurate evaluating of external feedback.

Here's an example of the impact S.A.T.s have on the feedback process:

Mary Casey, a medical director, is responsible for following up on staff complaints about physician behavior. One day Frank Jones, the director of nursing, informs her that, in spite of several attempts to correct the situation, Dr. Queeg, chief of surgery, continues to act in a "dictatorial and demanding manner" toward the surgical nurses.

The medical director enters the doctor's lounge the next morning and finds Dr. Queeg having a cup of coffee before beginning the day's surgeries. The medical director grabs a cup and pulls up a chair. Then she initiates the following interaction: "Listen Sam, before you head off to the wars today, I need you to do me a favor. I know you're under stress these days, we all are—but let up on the nurses, will you? They say you're pushing them so hard that they are running out of patience." Dr. Queeg rises from his chair and says, "Thanks, Mary. I'll take care of it."

What the medical director doesn't hear is the conversation going off in Dr. Queeg's head. In fact, Dr. Queeg does act in a "dictatorial and demanding way." In his mind, surgeons are superior to nurses, professionally speaking. It's likely that the giver's feedback triggered S.A.T.s in his mind. When Mary said "Let up on the nurses," Dr. Queeg heard, "Those damn nurses are complaining again." It is likely that the rest of what Mary said, including her attempt at empathy ("we're all under stress"), got blocked from his consciousness. All he heard was a tape that assured him that he, the chief of surgery, doesn't need some damn nurses telling him how to behave. No doubt the tape was booming in his mind—just as he would be booming when he stormed into the operating room to "take care of it."

As a result of self-talk, what is being evaluated in a receiver's mind may not be what the giver said or intended. To guard against such miscommunications, givers need to take responsibility for getting receivers to paraphrase their understanding of feedback. A feedback message isn't delivered—the Exchanging phase isn't over—until the receiver can convince the giver he or she "got it."

Whether receivers decide to act upon the words they correctly understood is a different matter. The key to the win-win exchange is the receiver's ability and willingness, during the Evaluating phase,

to explore how his own internal tapes may be distorting the conclusions drawn from the feedback.

The Source of S.A.T.s

Our minds are more powerful than any computer. Data that are neutral in their emotional charge (usually *describes* such as phone numbers and addresses) get filed away in certain portions of our
memories. Emotionally charged inputs, such as spankings from parents or humiliating experiences in school, are recorded in different
memory files. Like a thermostat, our mind does not distinguish positive situations from negative ones. It accepts and records them all
into our memories, although some are placed deeper than others
and are harder to access.

The nonjudgmental quality of our internal recorders explains
why high praise can trigger a flood of negative self-talk. (As the following section points out, the same nonjudgmental quality will turn
out to be a valuable asset.) As far as our minds are concerned,
intense *appreciates*—criticisms or praises—are all the same.

Consider how difficult it is for some people to say "thank you"
to positive *appreciates*. (Saying "thank you" is an *appreciate* in
return.) When a giver praises a receiver, she may get back a string
of *describes* that sound as if the receiver were trying to beat off a
compliment with a stick: "I had a lot of help." "I've been doing it
for years." "There was nothing to it." All of these statements may
be true, but they also suggest to the giver that their praise has made
the receiver feel uncomfortable.

Gracefully accepting feedback lets givers know that their comments have been heard and makes them more likely to compliment
receivers in the future—a real win-win. Gracefully accepting feedback from others begins with being able to give balanced feedback
to ourselves. S.A.T.s that cause receivers to fidget and get red in the
face when praised prevent them from recharging their own emotional batteries.

When it comes to self-talk, the brain cannot make an image of negative concepts. It can not picture words such as *none, never,* and *nowhere* (Hooper and Teresi, 1986). To clarify this vital point, try a sixty-second self-talk feedback exercise. Imagine eating an ice cream cone of your favorite flavor. Then, because you are so health conscious (and because one of your parents' feedback tapes echoes in your mind), you brush your teeth as soon as the cone is finished. Give it a go. Notice how the ice cream begins to drip down the cone, and feel yourself savoring the taste. Close your eyes and "see" these images in your mind four times. Now try to imagine yourself not eating an ice cream cone. What is the first image that flashed across your mind's eye?

When Michael Jordan steps up to the foul line for two shots, with his team down by a point and no time remaining on the game clock, he is not prescribing to himself, "Don't you miss!" Rather, he knows that he will make it, just as he did a hundred times in practice. He can see his teammates grin; he can hear the crowd roar as he makes the shots. His internal tape is positive; it is not neutral or negative.

There are two reasons why this is the case. One, as we just demonstrated, the mind can't visualize not doing something. It can visualize "missing it" and it can visualize "making it," but the command "Don't miss!" does not compute. (Makes us wonder about all the times we told our children, "Don't spill your milk!") Two, if the last message you give yourself before taking the action is "Don't miss," the last word your memory has processed and stored is the word "miss," and it is that word, that energy, that launches the ball.

Changing the Tape

The conversations in our minds are similar to our conversations with others. Both will require skillful use of ABCs to produce win-win outcomes. How many times has the critic that resides in each of our minds talked us out of doing something our hearts felt was the right thing to do and left us feeling demotivated as a result?

How many times have we heard the same back-and-forth argument—"I should, but . . . I shouldn't, but . . . "— taking place in our minds that left us feeling exhausted by the incessant debate? If internal conversations never seem to be successfully resolved, it is likely that the dialogue is suffering from an overuse, underuse, or misuse of the ABCs styles. The challenge in the Evaluating phase is the same: Can we re-create or replay the dialogue and then code it to see where or how to improve the exchange process? Can we make up our minds to change some of the tapes that make up our minds?

Changing old S.A.T.s can be daunting. First we must accept that these feedback tapes exist and understand how they work. When current circumstances resemble events that occurred when the tape was first made, the recorder's on button gets pushed. Next, each of us must learn to recognize the sound of a taped message and push the pause button. If it plays for too long, the listener becomes mesmerized by an old message—one that isn't in his best interest.

It would be nice if all we had to do was erase old tapes or throw them away. Obviously, we can't. But we can manage our S.A.T.s. rather than being imprisoned by them. To free our minds from the constant replaying of oldies that are not such goodies, we need to leverage the two ways that memories are created. A memory can be created by something others said or did to us or by messages we choose to play into our own memories, ourselves. The process used to create the memory makes no difference in the impact of the memory.

Silencing the Negative Inner Voice

Every time we hear a negative inner voice that is abusing or depreciating our self-esteem, we must not let it go on; we must respond. We must give it some feedback. This does not mean we ignore our faults but rather that we learn, through the feedback we give ourselves, to appreciate them along with our assets.

The first step is to code the conversation—to examine our ABCs Behavioral Compass—and label both the styles of feedback we've been giving ourselves and our typical responses. And then, as is true of every conflict interaction that is somehow stuck in a groove, the individual must accept the responsibility to alter her "normal" voice if she hopes to alter the other person's "typical" responses.

Let's look at a simple example. If a person's self-*appreciates* are always of the "constructive criticism" type—"You sure sounded flat during that speech!"—she can balance this internal *push* dialogue by pulling in some empathy, by consoling herself: "Couldn't have been too easy getting up for a speech after a six-hour plane delay." She can also add some positive *push* to balance the negative *push* by pointing out to herself one positive thing she did: "The beginning was flat, and I got a real rise with cartoons I used." If her self-talk is full of *describes* as to why something "won't work," she can add a few equally logical reasons why it "just might work." Ambiguous self-inflicted *prescribes*—"You should try harder!"—can be balanced by asking herself for a specific example of something more she could do. The forms a dialogue can take in our minds are no less varied than those we carry on with others.

The notion of self-talk sometimes falls into the mind-over-matter debate. Many factors influence the quality of our lives. Believers use positive self-affirmations because they see results, so we need not debate whether the results are real or imagined. However, on one point there can be no debate: The quality of our relationships cannot improve until the typical dialogue being exchanged is improved. This is equally true whether the dialogue is between myself and another or myself and a significant other who lives within me.

As Anaïs Nin said, "We don't see things as they are. We see things as we are." This statement is key to the power of evaluating how we evaluate the feedback we receive.

If we are to know who we are, we must seek, listen to, and understand feedback from others. We must do the same with the feedback we provide to ourselves. Rising to these challenges has very little to do with our intellectual abilities. Accepting who we are requires courage. It means taking personal responsibility for the S.A.T.s in our minds. Continuous quality improvement at the personal level demands our looking into the shadow sides of ourselves, accepting those shadows, and resolving to change.

7

Leadership and Feedback

In Chapters Three through Six, we took the Four-Phase Feedback model apart and examined each phase in detail. In Chapters Seven and Eight, we will look at how these concepts and tools relate to the real world.

A recent safari to Africa by Irv Rubin and his wife, Nan, included a visit to a Masai village. In no time at all Nan had a string of smiling young faces anxiously awaiting the pencil sketches of them that she was producing as fast as she could. All of this excitement caught the village chief's eye, and the next thing we knew his seven-foot frame was peering over Nan's shoulder. A wide grin crossed his almost toothless face as he made it very clear with gestures (and either an *ask* or a *prescribe* in Swahili) that his sketch was next.

Nan turned from the children and, with a bit more deliberation, made her sketch. Moments later, she handed him her best sixty-second feedback effort and looked nervously at Irv. The chief held it at arm's length, stared at it for a second, and then got a visibly upset look on his face. An animated and spirited spinning of his ABCs compass (Swahili style) passed between him and his highly educated son, who was serving as translator for the village. Nan and Irv laughed as his son explained, "My father has never seen a reflection of his face before. He didn't know what had happened to his teeth!"

We do not know whether the Masai chief ever looked in the behavioral mirror that appears when someone else provides him feedback. We do know that the chiefs in formal organizations face the challenge of getting accurate and honest feedback from others. What bosses most often get in the way of feedback is what an employee thinks the boss wants to hear. As a result, their opportunities for personal growth are limited. This personal loss is small compared to the potential consequences for the entire organization. Chief executive officers (CEOs) are supposed to lead by example, and if the standard they set is not win-win, the entire organization will lose.

If you are one of the chiefs, your decisions influence the lives of many people. Anyone familiar with organizational politics recognizes that the decisions leaders make are regularly based on incomplete information. In organizations where people fear their bosses, they hesitate to tell the truth. As information flows up the organizational hierarchy, it gets sanitized, and so, as a result, the boss seldom knows the whole truth. This chapter articulates some of the ways the dynamics of positional power interact with the ingredients that go into win-win relationships.

We are all aware that certain role relationships carry the weight of unspoken, powerful rules. From the time we are born, our parents use verbal and nonverbal feedback to teach us to comply with their definitions of right versus wrong, to implant their temperature settings into our being. For many children, these feedback exchanges result in their learning to "speak only when spoken to," or to "never disagree with an adult."

As children grow, these implanted rules of feedback broaden in scope and sharpen in their prescriptive focus. For example, visiting a doctor's office might result in one of these rules suggesting, "If the doctor wanted you to know, she would have told you." As we move through our professional careers, these childhood rules expand further: "If the boss wanted me to know, he would have told me," "Don't rock the boat, or you may be the one thrown overboard."

Little wonder when we hear the revised golden rule—"those who control the gold get to make the rules"—we come to believe that organizational honesty is primarily a one-way street.

Public and private sector leaders frequently misuse the exchange process we've been calling feedback. Government officials "apologize" for ethical mistakes, get their hands slapped as a consequence, and then win reelection from their peers. Employees withhold bad news or spin it in a more positive light. They justify their actions by arguing, quite appropriately, that anything else just wouldn't be politic. Long-gone messengers or whistle-blowers are part of an organization's oral history. Newcomers are told, "We don't disagree with the boss in public here." Many employees have suffered public ridicule and scathing criticism that their bosses, in the guise of just being honest, chose as constructive criticism of a new idea.

Still other bosses take pride in their bluntness. They do not understand the destructiveness of a tactless tongue. Sharpness without compassion hurts. Honesty of this nature is used to disguise a multitude of corporate sins from verbal abuse to the "that's-just-business-ethics" rationalization. We are beginning to realize that harassment comes in many forms, but the bottom line is the same: any behavior that is disrespectful of another person's self-esteem is bad behavior (Autry, 1991, pp. 118–120).

The Shock of Obedience

In a late 1960s documentary film, *Studies in Social Obedience*, shot in a laboratory in the basement of Yale University, a man (later identified as a dean at Yale) sobs uncontrollably as he follows an experimenter's instructions to flick switches on a huge electronic board. The sobbing man believed that these forty switches, labeled from fifteen to four hundred volts, were connected to electrodes taped to another person's chest. In an effort to speed up the learning process, increasingly strong electrical jolts were administered as feedback every time a wired subject gave the wrong answer to a question. In reality the sobbing man had been, himself, given a fifteen-volt jolt earlier, just to see how it felt. Additional feedback came in the form of screams presumed to be emanating from the person strapped to the electric chair in an adjoining room.

Milgram (1995) shocked us all when he proved that blind obedience to positional power, which drove millions to the gas chambers in World War II, was a human trait, not just a German one. Between one-third and one-half of random groups of subjects absolved themselves of responsibility, many while also sobbing uncontrollably at what they presumably had done. The subjects' postexperimental explanations for causing such harm included familiar rationalizations such as, "My boss told me to do it" or "I was just doing my job."

Few subjects resisted their white-coated leaders, who were presented as esteemed university professors. A small percentage did try to exercise their feedback muscles by arguing that no amount of human pain was worth any research findings, not to mention the $5.00 in compensation they received. They were quickly and easily brought into line with a series of "authoritative" pushes back including, "This experiment could benefit mankind" or "You agreed to complete this experiment" or, the clincher, "I [the professor] will take responsibility for anything that happens."

Ash (1995) added another feedback-related dynamic in his landmark studies of the development of group norms, the unwritten standards to which people adhere to avoid being ostracized. Ash believed that social pressure to conform to majority views of what was right would lead people to deny their own experience of reality, to deny their own perceptions of the truth. And he was right! In one series of experiments, the presumed results of a poll of people's beliefs about the U.S. Constitution were flashed up on a screen. As a result, for example, thirty-three percent of large samples of responsible citizens agreed that "freedom of speech was a privilege that could be revoked at will." In a second series of experiments—instead of using impersonal polls—Ash decided to increase the feeling of social pressure by forming small groups. Three-to-four-person groups were formed, each made up of one naive subject and the rest paid helpers who had been told exactly how to behave. Thirty-three to fifty percent of the experimental subjects misperceived the length of two parallel lines; lines so obviously different that solitary, unpressured control subjects never misperceived them! For the question of which line was longer, the feedback given by those in the experimentally manipulated hot seat typically followed the norm (the standard of correctness) that had been created by the opinion of the two to three paid conspirators in the group.

In the postexperimental debriefing, everyone admitted to having made a mistake as to the length of the two lines. Explanations ranged from circumstantial ("I had a bad angle") to more worrisome, self-effacing rationalizations ("I know it's time for me to get my contact lenses checked"). Keep in mind that the errors in judgment took place in groups of strangers without the human bonds we'd expect to develop in organizations or families. Nothing of any emotional or financial significance was at stake. Rocking the boat—going against the group norm—would not cost a person a salary increase, a promotion, a job, or even someone's friendship.

The results of these two experiments can be easily applied to the real world of someone in a position of power who can say, "Pull the switch."

In the Real World

When Tom Campbell was a practicing gynecologist, he did complete medical histories and physical exams on all new patients. After he finished the history, he would ask his patient to don one of the gowns piled on the table, explaining that he would return shortly to conduct the physical exam. Because he was very concerned about his patients' comfort, he'd decided to never use the inexpensive Kleenex paper–type gowns. The higher cost and laundering expense of short linen gowns seemed small in comparison to the patient's increased comfort. As he left the room one day, he nodded toward the pile on the table and said to his patient, "Please put one of those on; I'll be back shortly." He returned and was stunned to find his patient wearing nothing, save the pillow case pulled over her head. The laundry had inadvertently returned it with the pile of gowns.

The same feedback-related dynamics that led Ash's subjects to "go along with the majority," Milgram's subjects to "push the switch," and the patient to pull the pillowcase over her eyes also led members of President Kennedy's administrative cabinet in the early 1960s to withhold data from being introduced during the tense discussions concerning the Cuban Missile Crisis. Esteemed public servants, imperfect human beings sworn to act for the benefit and security of the entire nation, consciously and willfully withheld vital feedback. Rather than risk their own security in the group and possibly incur the president's displeasure, key cabinet members chose not to tell the president everything they knew about Cuba's readiness to launch an atomic attack. The power of group think and the fear of providing feedback the boss may not want to hear are not by any means dynamics that occur only in laboratory basements of universities (Janus, 1995).

Readers who have been in the U.S. military will appreciate the following example for its dissimilarity to readers' own experience. During 1973, shortly after the end of the six-day war in the Middle East Irv Rubin visited Israel. He observed an Israeli military unit planning for a raid.

Every idea, regardless of the position held by its proponent, went through the same gut-wrenching scrutiny. Feedback flew hot and heavy in every direction. The commanding officer's ideas often got shot down but, on the other hand, fewer Israeli soldiers did. The soldiers recognized that unwillingness to be a messenger bearing bad news could result in people getting killed, so everyone spoke up.

Imagine Rubin's shock when, after several years' consulting experience with the U.S. Navy, he realized that in the Israeli military—during planning exercises—there was no correlation between people's behavior and the number of stripes on their shirts.

Boardroom Dynamics

Let us take a closer look at the subtle ways these feedback dynamics might manifest themselves in the boardroom. Remember the story of the emperor's new clothes? The first thing we learn about Andersen's unclad emperor is that he suffered from a disease common among those who have risen to the top. "He couldn't be bothered with his soldiers . . . or . . . with going out . . . except to show off his new clothes" (Ash and Higton, 1992, pp. 14–21). Like many of his modern-day counterparts who often send a feedback signal to their secretaries to tell callers they are in a meeting, the emperor, it was said, was always "in wardrobe."

By contrast, seasoned ex-CEOs such as James Autry are urging us to develop caring leadership, made up of emperors who recognize that the "learning of leadership begins as an interior process, the first step of which is self-awareness" (Autry, 1994, p. 39). Autry points out that the opposite belief seems to characterize the lion's share of corporate America whose "managers will change organization structure, systems, employees—anything at all except themselves. Then they wonder why the fix hasn't worked. Their attitude is supremely arrogant, without self-awareness, introspection or humility" (Autry, 1994, p. 48).

Corporate senior executives, like the Masai chief and Andersen's emperor, will find it very difficult to enhance their own self-awareness without feedback from others, without holding themselves up to undistorted mirrors. To paraphrase George Bernard Shaw, progress is impossible without change, and those who cannot change their minds cannot change anything.

One of the prevailing mind-sets that Autry says has to change is the role accorded the "touchy-feely stuff" in feedback exchanges between leaders and their followers. Autry goes right to the heart of every macho chief's fears and suggests that leaders should not just feel okay about crying but see it as an absolutely appropriate and necessary emotion to express at work. Crying is nothing more than a human emotion, and, with one exception, all human emotion—displeasure, irritation, disappointment, unbridled enthusiasm, and so on—need to be expressed directly with sensitivity and compassion. The one exception to this array is anger, which, when expressed in an abusive and demeaning manner, "frequently leads to humiliation, and humiliation is the one thing no employee will ever forgive you. Management without emotional hiding places—where feedback is exchanged regularly, flowing both uphill and down—is the most difficult management there is" (Autry, 1991, pp. 108–109).

Andersen's naked emperor also reminds us of the danger of our reliance on false fronts. The need to wear a mask, to clothe our true feelings in the threads of a self-woven gilded persona, is the breeding ground of hubris—the very hubris that enabled the swindlers who arrived on the scene to play on the emperor's worst fears. Their promise to the emperor that, with his new clothes, he would be able immediately to "find out who in [the] kingdom is no good at his job . . . to be able to tell the bright ones from the stupid ones" was too much to resist. Imagine being a leader—one of those who sees expressing emotion to an employee as a sign of weakness—and not having to rely upon emotionally messy procedures such as performance appraisals and feedback discussions!

Special uniforms or not, CEOs never get to the top without checking on suppliers, without covering their flanks. So our emperor decided to send his trusted and "honest old minister over to the weavers . . . for he's bright and no one attends to his job better than he." And, just to be safe, he sent another trusted official a few weeks later. Both fell into the trap of self-doubt our egos set for us all the time. Unspoken fears, caused by the emptiness before their eyes when the crooked weavers showed them how the emperor's golden thread had been put to use, raised a flood of questions: "Could it be that I'm no good at my job? Could it be that I'm stupid?" Their self-talk fears were quickly assuaged by the distorted feedback they gave to their CEO as to how absolutely ravishing he would look in his new clothes.

This positional power feedback dynamic culminates when the emperor decides to see for himself what's going on. But instead of going to look by himself, he brings an entourage, including his two trusted aides—the same two loyal subjects who had already publicly advertised (and, like Ash's experimental subjects, been paid for) their votes. Even the emperor couldn't go against the tide of group conformity, and no one else in his domain would commit political suicide. The vote was a unanimous "beautiful, gorgeous, splendid!"—until a child who was taught rules of feedback different from those most of us have learned blurted the truth: "But he hasn't got anything on!"

The last few lines of the story poignantly document the power of needing to save face, even if it's only a false persona: "And the people whispered the child's words to one another until at last the whole populace roared. 'But he hasn't anything on!' The emperor felt his blood turn cold, for he sensed they were right, but he thought to himself, 'I must go through with the procession now.' And the lords-in-waiting walked after him, carrying the train that simply wasn't there."

Senior managers and emperors are human beings; they are not mind readers. Without feedback, they cannot learn, and they have no choice but to repeat unhelpful behaviors and consequently affect others in less-than-desirable ways. In addition, their decisions are, by definition, meant to affect the lives of many others for a long time to come. Therefore, when something turns out badly for us or for an organization, instead of pointing the finger of blame at our leaders, all staff need to look in the mirror and ask themselves, "Am I not—in part—a victim of my own unwillingness to speak the truth as I see it?"

360-Degree Feedback Can Be an Alternative, If . . .

In Chapter One we labeled 360-degree feedback—as it is normally approached, anonymous and averaged—as the equivalent of "going around in circles." You have every right, therefore, to be wondering what we'd prescribe as an alternative way to fulfill the need for honest feedback. A partial answer to this question comes from people who have used their ABCs Behavioral Compasses to successfully manage the feedback process. As a part of the 360-degree experience, participants take personal responsibility to collect and analyze direct, nonanonymous feedback from samples of their own choosing. Every manager who has ever used this process included several direct reports in this sample.

In the feedback they are asked to provide, respondents (givers) can request more or less of five specific behaviors from a pool of forty-eight options. One of the specific *appreciate* behaviors included in these Temenos® feedback surveys (see Appendix) is, "[Manager] tells me [the participant seeking the feedback] specifically what he/she [the respondent] doesn't like about what I'm doing." It is shocking to most people to see their bosses check this specific behavior as one they'd like to see their employees exhibit more frequently!

In helping people deal with their surprise and anxiety over the prospect of telling their bosses specifically how they—the bosses—might improve, we offer them the following rhetorical *ask*: "Would you ever think of asking someone to give you constructive criticism more frequently if you did not respect that person and his or her opinion?" As people think about this question, they come to realize the incongruity and fundamental lack of integrity implicit in expecting people to be honest with them if they themselves feel hesitant to be honest with their bosses. We don't agree with Hal Lancaster, who states that such direct feedback increases "managers' concerns about it undermining authority" (Lancaster, 1996, p. 1); we believe it reflects a growing desire to humanize the workplace.

We believe win-win feedback can enable bosses and subordinates to become more mutually responsive.

It is indeed lonely at the top—but a moment's reflection leads us to realize that we are all at the top. In the business of living, we are all CEOs. We are responsible and accountable for the feedback we give others and ourselves and what we decide to do about it.

A Temenos® client has taken the ABCs behaviors and integrated them into his organization's heart and soul. We've asked that organization's leaders to share their D.A.P.s directly with readers, which they do in Chapter Eight. In closing, consider these words by Deng Ming-Dao (1992, p. 93):

> Truth perceived gives assurance.
> Skill yields self-reliance.
> With courage we can defy danger.
> To increase power, increase humility.

8

. . . .

Evolutionary Change with
Revolutionary Effects
A Case Study

Our primary focus thus far has been on the vital role feedback plays in the growth and learning of individuals. In this chapter, the focus shifts in two ways. The first shift is to organizations, which are communities of individuals who are the learning entities of organizations. Through individuals' efforts to learn through feedback, organizations will grow and develop—or not. The most familiar formal mechanism through which individual learning is transformed into organizational growth is the process of performance appraisal. This chapter, therefore, focuses on how a unique pediatric medical practice is using the formal performance appraisal process and a feedback tool called The Behavior Minder® in its efforts to create an organizational culture dedicated to excellence in patient care.

A word about our emphasis on *how* is necessary before proceeding. In the world of high-technology medicine, without the most careful pre-op preparation and post-op care, the body could easily reject the transplanted heart it needs for its very survival. The same is true of any major organizational intervention. As a high-technology tool, The Behavior Minder® can support the creation of a high-touch, healing-oriented organizational culture, the soil from which excellence in patient care grows (Rubin and Fernandez, 1991). To become the heart and soul of such a new organizational paradigm, it will have to touch the lives of each and every employee. *How* the transplantation process of this tool is handled will ultimately determine the success of the operation.

As a result, there is an unseen, unrecognized, and unappreciated level of dirty work with respect to the "how" question that leaders of organizational culture change can never delegate. It is non-negotiable. They must lead by example. Their day-to-day behavior must serve as a model for others to follow. Without this quality, organizational culture change can have no integrity. The case study that follows directly addresses this issue.

The second shift readers will experience in this chapter is that of the voice they hear: from those of the authors to that of Teresa Lever. As the then COO—and recently, the CEO—of Nightime Pediatrics, Teresa agreed—on behalf of Nightime's President, Dr. Rod Pollary, and on behalf of the 120 dedicated employees and the seventy-five thousand children they care for seven days a week from 5:00 P.M. until midnight—to share her personal experiences with the vital role day-to-day feedback plays in providing excellence in patient care. We are grateful for her honesty and courage.

Nightime Pediatric Clinics: A Case Study

The following paragraphs tell the story in Teresa's words.

The Presenting Symptoms

Organizations, like the humans that comprise them, experience life phases of birth, infancy, adolescence, and so on. For Nightime Pediatric Clinics [NPC], adolescence began in early 1993. Managers were finding themselves increasingly unable to handle the escalation and intensity of interpersonal conflicts among the staff. Like real teenagers rebelling against authority figures, NPC's employees were not interested in honest feedback from me, from any other supervisors, or from one another.

One senior physician claimed to have the best interests of Nightime at heart as the reason for his letter of resignation as a site medical director. He said that, even if it meant predominately working out of other clinics, he wanted never again to be scheduled to work alongside a particular physician colleague whose parent and patient interactions and effect on employee morale was, in the letter writer's opinion, a liability to Nightime.

My long-term vision for NPC had been to create healthy life experiences—experiences that enhance and nurture self-esteem—for all its employees. There is no doubt in my mind that healthy employees help patients get more healthy. The day-to-day behaviors of many of NPC's personnel were anything but healthy, and, as a consequence, I found myself working nights and weekends to find the right answer.

By now, doctors who were becoming quite impatient with the lack of worker harmony (while owning none of the responsibility themselves) were threatening to leave. In an attempt to satisfy them, Dr. Pollary and I worked to create a new compensation system. In return for what we thought was a generous productivity-based package, we asked physicians to affirm their commitment to NPC by signing an employment contract. (Looking back, I realize that I deluded myself into believing the medical staff's feedback when they told me that the new compensation program was terrific. Two days later, I discovered that they were slandering our efforts behind our backs.)

Dr. Pollary and I have always believed in open, honest, face-to-face feedback. I already knew that my staff had been less than fully honest with me, so I was not completely surprised to receive a letter—resulting from

a series of secret meetings—that summarized physicians'
feelings:

*In the course of these meetings, it became readily evident that
[we agreed that] an inordinate amount of time and energy
expenditures had been devoted to the development of the
compensation system, the employee handbook, the pediatri-
cian's orientation manual, and the delineation of Nightime's
mission. . . .*

*What also became clear was the fact that much of the
policy, procedure and administrative approach to physician
and patient issues emanated from nonmedical personnel,
thereby creating a major source of frustration to all of the
physicians who are the cornerstone of Nightime's operation.*

*It also seemed clear to all that, because the mission of
Nightime Pediatrics is patient care, the administration of
Nightime at all levels ought to involve the physicians who
are primarily responsible for such care.*

*Therefore, the regular physicians are suggesting that the
MEDICAL STAFF* [emphasis in original] *assume responsibility for policies, procedures and administrative issues affecting physicians, physician-staff relationships, physician-patient
relationships and all aspects of patient care. By so doing,
the medical staff could relieve you of a large portion of your
administrative burden, which the rest of us (many of whom
have had broad and sufficient administrative experience to
help you) could handle on your behalf.*

I got the message: the doctors were planning to unseat
me. I needed a miracle.

Diagnosis and Treatment Plan

A few days later, I was spending yet another Saturday sitting alone in my office, silently contemplating the joys
of "packing it all in" when the cover of a book I'd

ordered weeks earlier caught my eye. I spent the next two hours reading My *Pulse Is Not What It Used to Be* [Rubin and Fernandez, 1991]. As a result, I learned that NPC was not sick; it was merely suffering growing pains. The company needed to move through the normal evolutionary challenges to grow into an organization in search of excellence, as NPC's mission demanded and as its patients deserved. I asked Dr. Pollary to read the book immediately, and the next day we called Irv and struck up what has been for all of us an extraordinary relationship.

Several naive misconceptions I had were dispelled early on in this relationship. A checklist of issues that need to be addressed by organizations to help them determine their readiness, motivation, and capability to embark on the never-ending journey in search of excellence warned that "it is safe to say an organization cannot earmark too much time and money from training budgets" (Rubin and Fernandez, 1991, p. 20). At the time, NPC faced a potential loss of several hundred thousand dollars and a workforce resistant to any "touchy-feely" styles of communication. But Dr. Pollary supported the process and substantially increased Nightime's investment in training and development over the next few years. (Responding to intense unrest with this investment decision, in a memo to employees Dr. Pollary invited those who could not "support and sustain each other in the effort to do our best" to leave Nightime.)

Furthermore, I should have realized sooner that no single thing we did as senior management to manage our brainchild—from new structures to a plethora of organizational manuals and policies—would quell the discontent rumbling throughout our organization. . . . Never again will I lull myself into believing in the easier, softer way in which I see most organizations approaching the challenges of TQM-oriented culture change. . . . Before we can expect to sequentially create the new bricks to which Rubin and Fernandez refer—the organizational blocks of mission, structures, and procedures, all intended to shape and alter behavior—we must first learn new behaviors. We have to re-engineer the re-engineers before the culture of the organization can be re-engineered!

I believe this is true of all organizations, particularly in health care, where quality is a three-legged stool supported by technical effectiveness, managerial efficiency, and day-to-day interpersonal efficacy [Rubin, 1992; Rubin and Inguagiato, 1990]. I have learned that organizational culture is synonymous with day-to-day behavior. So unless observable, day-to-day behavior changed over time—beginning with NPC's senior managers— NPC's culture couldn't have changed.

In the aftermath of all the turmoil that came to a head after the physicians' letter, Nightime renewed its approach to the challenge of holding itself and all its employees accountable and responsible for the win-win quality of their day-to-day behaviors.

The Prescription

Irv Rubin recommended that NPC implement The Behavior Minder®, an innovative interactive program he invented [see Appendix]. The program is designed to support continuously the creation of the win-win, healing-oriented organizational culture Nightime required. At the stroke of a key on any one of our computers, each and every NPC employee can be made aware of her or his behavior and its day-to-day consequences on co-workers. A user-friendly way to get "360-degree feedback 365 days a year" was, in my view, the managerial information system NPC had always lacked. With The Behavior Minder® in place, all could now be held accountable for managing the quality of their many important day-to-day relationships. The Behavior Minder® would, I believed, empower NPC with the ABCs of effective feedback needed to develop the win-win relationships upon which quality patient care rests.

To provide one example of how this tool can be used, I'd like to invite you to "sit in" on a meeting that took place in 1995 between myself and Nightime's then newly appointed medical director, Dr. Ken Broadbent. (One of the structural changes NPC had to make was to relieve Dr. Pollary of one of his many hats, that of medical director.)

An Intentional Compass

Ken's and my relationship was strained, to say the least, in the way that so many relationships were at NPC. Communication between us was becoming stilted, skewed, guarded, and frustrating. Working together felt like more trouble than it was worth. I had serious doubts as to if and how the relationship could continue. I soon learned that Ken was feeling the same way.

Just before I was readying to do the same, Ken initiated the idea that he and I talk out our dynamics. (The integrity and courage it took to do that were among the very qualities that attracted me to him as my medical director in the first place.) To prepare for this meeting, each of us had a few simple tasks to complete. Before we went through the steps involved in entering data into our computers, however, we made an explicit and important emotional agreement. We agreed on how we wanted to feel about one another and ourselves at the end of our interaction. It was critical to both of us that we be able to say we'd been completely honest and treated one another with respect and integrity. This setting of an "intentional compass" helped us to proceed.

Using our new computerized program, we proceeded to enter our individual perceptions of the frequency with which each of us exhibited each of forty-eight win-win behaviors in our relationship. (The Behavior Minder® is designed to guarantee individual user anonymity. No one but me could see the feedback Ken gave me and vice versa.) In addition, we had to identify five specific behaviors each wished the other would exhibit more frequently or less frequently to strengthen the quality of the relationship. Then, working separately in the privacy of our own offices, we reviewed the feedback we'd received from the other person before getting together to discuss the results. (Although it is a computerized program, The Behavior Minder® does not eliminate or substitute for face-to-face feedback but rather it facilitates the process. Using summarized, anonymous, one-way data—as is the case with most 360-degree feedback tools today—has always seemed to me to violate the fundamental rule that every relationship is a two-way street.)

Ken and I both approached our meeting with anxiety. As a result, we manufactured a succession of justifiable task-related excuses for having to postpone meeting and looking into the relationship-oriented mirror The Behavior Minder® affords. But once we got started, the results were quite extensive. After three hours, Ken and I had barely scratched the surface!

The many discrepancies we discovered between our intentions, our awareness of our own behaviors and their consequences, immediately explained the growing sense of loneliness and isolation we'd been experiencing. Instead of confirming our worst fears of mutual uncaring, we found that exactly the opposite was true. Each of us, with the best of intentions, had been doing everything possible to show the other how much we cared! But both Ken and I had been acting out of relative ignorance. Assumptions had taken on the air of facts. In particular, we'd each assumed the other's needs were identical to our own. We'd never asked each other which specific behaviors each needed to experience to feel cared for by the other.

With this experience under my belt, I felt a surge of optimism as I planned to integrate The Behavior Minder® into NPC's formal performance appraisal process.

A New Behavioral Ethic

Performance appraisal is how an organization holds itself accountable for the specific behaviors it espouses as necessary to achieve excellence. All talk about what's important in any organization rests on what is measured and the consequences of meeting (or not meeting) those standards. My first challenge in getting NPC ready to accept the use of The Behavior Minder® has gone through several steps.

Step One: Beginning with Myself; Leading by Example In the late fall of 1995 and early spring of 1996, I began using The Behavior Minder® with my twelve direct reports as a part of their yearly performance appraisals. Rather than the general discussions about leadership, teamwork, communication and the like that had characterized previous appraisals, The Behavior Minder® would allow us to focus on the specific concrete behaviors that underlie these abstract qualities. The only data involved this first time through the process were the perceptions we shared of one another.

I met with each of these people for a minimum of two hours. In retrospect, I am convinced that my preparation for these sessions was vital to their success. I knew that my modeling of win-win behaviors was going to be the most important tool I had to call upon in these interactions. I felt a heavy responsibility to have the healthiest interactions I could, feeling very much like a surgeon about to perform an open heart transplant! (In my case, therefore, a significant part of my preparation involved asking God for the strength to do the best job I was capable of.)

I was amazed, as were the other participants, at how easily these one-on-one performance appraisal meetings went. The first half of each meeting was spent sharing and discussing The Behavior Minder® we had exchanged. I believe The Behavior Minder® helped us to build a relationship based on mutual understanding. The stage was then set so that my staff could now handle with ease the sometimes difficult task-related issues that are a part of a formal performance appraisal discussion. The impersonal nature of the computer provided a safe doorway for getting through the fear of directly giving and receiving feedback.*

Step Two: Moving to the Next Level; Repeating the Process
I next gave my management team colleagues the task of replicating—with their teams—the process I had experienced with them. I mistakenly assumed that because they and I had such a healthy first experience, moving forward

---

*A sample of the hard-copy feedback reports available to a fictitious employee named Bill based on feedback from his fictitious colleague, John, appears in the Appendix.

would be easy for them. The fear and resistance they voiced helped me to see immediately that being receivers of the process and having to be the deliverers were not the same thing. I knew it didn't make any sense to require someone who was fearful to implement the tool.

I called upon my Human Resource Department for help. I knew I could trust them—from both a training competence and alignment of values confidence viewpoint—to visit each of our clinics and teach people how The Behavior Minder® actually worked. The mechanics were obviously the easy part. Getting people over their unwarranted fears was the challenge, a challenge they have met with results I can only describe as terrific and fantastic.

As of this writing, spring 1997, I am preparing for my own second round of Behavior Minder®–supported performance appraisals. This time, however, I am extending the behavioral database for the discussions. We will continue to directly share our mutual perceptions and needs of one another. In addition, however, I have asked that my managers be prepared to bring along summaries of the five specific needs others have asked them to consider. (These summaries are printed out for them from their own computers. The anonymous nature of the individual relationships that go into making up these summary patterns will not be violated unless individuals themselves choose to do so!)

My objective is public and straightforward: to be certain that I am in a position, as their primary coach, to do anything I can to support my colleagues in our continuous quality improvement responsibilities—our need to continually improve the win-win quality of our day-to-day behaviors.

The Results

I believe that—in spite of the enormous gains we've realized already—the depth and richness of The Behavior Minder® as a feedback tool in the service of creating truly healing-oriented organizational cultures has yet to be fully revealed. As my NPC colleagues and I continue to grow and develop ourselves, I have no doubt we will create new and exciting ways to benefit from win-win feedback.

What the staff and doctors learned about each other has taken the entire organization to a higher level of mutual understanding. That understanding has fueled a more intense desire and level of commitment—to varying degrees among individuals—to the fact that feedback promotes growth and health. And if two healthy individuals with a commitment to mutual understanding and dialogue can do a lot of wonderful things together, an organization full of such individuals is absolutely unstoppable.

The communication process in general and the feedback process in particular is much healthier—less fear-driven, more open, and more comfortable—among all of NPC's staff, including its physicians. Having a senior physician, for example, consciously striving to incorporate NPC's win-win philosophies and principles into a newly designed patient feedback process is a far cry from the ultimatums that characterized their feedback experiences a few short years ago. In this same short period, we have learned that feedback can and must be given with care and concern—the keys to our business in the first place.

Clear and valuable examples have emerged where I can see the habit of win-win feedback influencing relationships with patients. In staff at all levels—from the front-line troops who deal with thousands of frightened parents weekly to those behind the lines who handle angry questions about billing—I can see an increased tenderness that fuels an understanding of and desire to receive feedback from patients.

At a more personal level, I feel rewarded by the win-win potential of the gift of feedback. I have always believed that the trials and tribulations experienced by Nightime as an organization (and my own family organization, as well) are a mirror into my own heart and soul. As I become stronger and healthier in my ability and willingness to meet these never-ending challenges, I sense that NPC becomes healthier and stronger as well.

9

Axioms and Tips

In Chapter Two, two aids were introduced to help reduce the fear of giving and receiving feedback. One was a map that enables you to locate where you are and where you need to be headed at any moment in the process. The second was a behavioral compass. Given that you know where you are and where you are headed, which behavioral course should you chart to help you reach your destination in a win-win manner?

In Chapters Three through Six, each of the four map locations—*Initiating, Formulating, Exchanging,* and *Evaluating*—and their relevant compass points were examined in detail. Then, in Chapters Seven and Eight, the focus shifted to how the pieces fit back together in two contexts. In the first case (Chapter Seven), we examined the unique feedback challenges facing those in positions of leadership. In the second case (Chapter Eight), we saw how one organization integrated the feedback process into its formal performance appraisal process as a way of creating and maintaining a win-win organizational culture.

If we, the authors, have done our jobs as givers, then you, the reader, our receiver, realize how important feedback is and how much room we all, givers and receivers alike, have for self-improvement. In a further effort to support your readiness and motivation to change, part of Chapter Six summarizes key ingredients of championship feedback. Here in Chapter Nine we intend to put the icing on that feedback. Of course, there is no foolproof recipe. Feedback is an exchange implemented by imperfect human beings, so it will be, by definition, an imperfect process. When the product is a process, progress—not perfection—is as good as the recipe gets.

Let's look at four axioms—rules of conduct we accept as self-evident truths. These axioms will sound familiar, but we believe they have to be reframed to fit the rules of conduct required by a win-win feedback exchange.

Our reconstructed axioms will focus on truths that can help address the question, What can *we* do when, regardless of how good our map or compass readings are, *we* find ourselves unsure how to proceed, or just plain lost? Our emphasis on the word *we* is meant to sensitize us all to the first and most fundamental axiom.

Axiom One: We Are All Different— in Very Similar Ways

The nature of the truths seen in any situation will be influenced by our human differences in general and our gender differences in particular. As an ancient Cheyenne teaching states, "Within every man there is a reflection of a woman, and within every woman there is a reflection of a man. Within every man and woman there is also the reflection of an old man and an old woman, a little boy and a little girl" (Roberts and Amidom, 1991). The fact that each of us is different—in some very similar ways—will influence how we use the feedback map and the ABCs Behavioral Compass. Differences notwithstanding, our common objective should be clear: in giving and receiving feedback, we must always do so with the utmost mutual respect and strive to recognize, appreciate, and learn from our differences.

Health care is a profession in which women and men work side by side under stressful life-and-death situations. Under these circumstances, nothing short of win-win relationships among all health care professionals is acceptable. To help begin sharpening our awareness of gender differences in behavior and their consequences, let's examine a stereotypical situation with a familiar ring. Tips will be offered to help us self-correct when our differences cause us to fall off the win-win feedback track.

A husband and wife are headed toward a new restaurant for dinner. The restaurant is so popular that it took four weeks to get their 7:00 P.M. reservation. By 7:15 P.M., it is obvious that the husband, who is driving, is lost. He mumbles a true but not terribly reassuring *describe:* "I know it's around here somewhere." The wife, intending to be helpful, offers a perfectly logical *prescribe* with an *ask* question at its tail: "Why don't you stop at that gas station and ask for directions?" Unless this couple has developed their relationship skills, their meal—when they finally get it—isn't the only thing likely to be steaming hot!

Gender differences are so pronounced it often appears we originated from different planets (Gray, 1992). We are, in fact, raised in different neighborhoods, and many of the gender-related behaviors we learn on playground monkey bars—as well as from climbing our own family trees—become fixed and automatic.

As a result of these early socialization experiences, a simple mechanical truth that transcends gender differences emerges. Our persons are pieces of extraordinarily sophisticated equipment that have been finely tuned through thousands of years of listening to feedback and learning from experience. As a result of our evolution, we are incredibly good listeners, although there are marked variations on how much we attend to what we've heard. At a semiconscious level, we are always picking up nuances in music and dance when significant others are giving us feedback.

Reflect further that the closer you are to a transmitter and the louder the verbal signals, the more likely they will register on you as a receiver. Consequently, the voice I am most familiar with and accustomed to hearing through my own ears is my own, regardless of gender.

As a result, most males are less likely to hear feelings being expressed, precisely because their ears are attuned to hearing the factual signals they have learned to express. Similarly, most women hear feelings because they have learned to communicate them. Furthermore, the differences in what we hear relate directly to the different ways we think and act. Men have been trained to be problem solvers. The faster they can solve a problem, the better they feel about themselves, and the better they assume the person in need will feel about them. When a woman expresses a feeling—"I've had another terrible day with my boss today"—a man will typically jump right in and prescribe a solution—"Maybe you should start looking for another job." At some point in the exchange, she may want prescriptive feedback that helps her to look at possible solutions. In the beginning, what she wants is someone who will serve as a sounding board without sounding bored! She wants to talk about what's bothering her for a while before thinking about solution-oriented feedback. (We urge the reader to remember we are speaking in familiar stereotypes because they are so pervasive and reflective of the communication challenges our gender differences engender.)

Rational *prescribes* from men in response to emotionally charged *describes* from women simply do not register for the same reasons that emotionally laden *prescribes* or rhetorical *asks* from women cause interpersonal static in men. Neither is at fault. Feedback that says "you're not communicating" is not true. The truth is, there is a problem that needs correction in the space between us. The transmission process, like feedback, relies on two distinct mechanical components—a sender and a receiver. Each of us is responsible for clearing up the static in our half of the exchange. A few more examples of such static should sound very familiar.

Women report that it is a source of great frustration when a man becomes mentally absent when confronted by emotionally charged feedback. Actually, he isn't absent at all; he is mulling over the best solution to the problem, a problem the woman wants to explore and talk about, not immediately resolve. To make matters worse, while intending to make them better, the more serious the problem sounds to him, the deeper he will retreat, because solutions to really bad problems are, by logical Martian definition, harder to find (Gray, 1992).

Conversely, men regularly throw their hands up in exasperation because they can not fathom why their counterparts from Venus seem unable to add any well-thought-out, rational *describes* to their spontaneous expressions of feelings. And his asking, "Why do you feel that way?" only throws oil on troubled waters. Even if a rational answer is forthcoming, his next move would likely be to springboard into a *prescribe* that fits the newly identified cause.

Consider another set of gender-related dynamics our earlier restaurant example suggests. For many reasons, men do not ask for help. To seek directions for getting to the restaurant (or for putting together a piece of equipment "so simple to assemble, even a child can do it") means two unacceptable things to most men: I am lost, and I have failed. Unsolicited, helpful *prescribes* with an *ask* at its tail from a woman—"Why don't you stop at the gas station and ask for directions?"—only aggravate his feelings of incompetence. An easier-to-swallow initiating step might be for her to ask, "Is there anything I can do to help at the moment?"

Sensitivity to the difference between prescribing and ascribing is vital. Being prescriptively assertive without sounding aggressive is a challenge for us all, particularly when we're under stress, such as when we're running late for something important. "I need for us to stop for a second and ask someone directions" would be a clear *prescribe*—a focus on needs versus what should or should not be done. In contrast, the feedback "You should have done . . . " will be heard as ascribing blame, as pointing the finger of responsibility at you, implying that you have caused the problem. In our restaurant scenario, therefore, in addition to the possible usefulness of an open-ended *ask* like the one just mentioned, a quick D.A.P. would also keep the steam down: "Neither one of us has ever been to this restaurant before." [*describe*] "Your sense of direction is usually right on." [*appreciate*] "How about we stop at that gas station and I'll run in and ask for directions?" [*prescribe*]

What we must also remember, despite our differences, is that we all have needs that have to be met. What differs is how we go about meeting the needs we share. Some of us simply use our *push* energy: we tell receivers directly what we need from them. Others have learned to use the *pull* energy: they ask someone what she needs or wants, in hopes of being asked to state their needs in return. The question "Do you want to go to the movies tonight?" carries an unspoken expectation of more than just a "no" response, end of conversation. The human rule of reciprocity is that the original question initiates a dialogue. An *ask* is more than simply an attempt to satisfy the human need for confirmation. It is often meant to satisfy our human need for affirmation, that our opinion—and therefore our person—is important enough to be responded to: "No, I don't. What do you want to do tonight?"

For illustrative purposes, we have emphasized our common gender differences. However, we cannot lose sight of the fact that we are unique individuals, regardless of gender. An effective feedback process requires both giver and receiver to recognize the inherent strength in the richness of these differences, for the whole can only be greater than the sum of the parts if we consciously integrate the disparate parts into one whole. The following list of ABCs compass tips—relevant to all of us—will help us to navigate through the feedback process and achieve such synergy in our interpersonal relationships.

- Follow the KISS principle when you *describe*: *keep it simple, stupid.*

- Be sure your *prescribe* does not ascribe.

- Avoid the rhetorical *ask* (a *prescribe* with a question mark).

- *Appreciate* your humanness; offer and accept apologies gracefully.

- When *attending* to someone, be fully present—this is the greatest gift we can offer.

- *Ask* abundantly—this is an act of affirmation and confirmation, not just a way of seeking information.

- Always check *understanding*.

- *Empathize* before you criticize or moralize.

This list, as we see, is a challenge for us to get perfect. This leads us to the next axiom.

Axiom Two: Practice Makes Permanent, So Make It Good Practice

We are all overwhelmed at times by learning effective feedback skills. Fortunately, we've got our entire lifetime to do it. In addition, there are proven tips to help us develop good practice.

- *Be prepared.* Think through the coming interaction and mentally practice being successful. Saying something that has been carefully prepared but is delivered without notes is very compatible with being spontaneous. You will have to add the ABCs music and dance of your feelings, at the moment, during the feedback exchange.

- *Use your instant replay button.* If, during an exchange, something doesn't feel right to you, ask for a momentary time out: "Give me a second, will you please?" Consult your internal coach. Mentally replay what just transpired. If you, as the giver or receiver, conclude that your behavior was off, getting back on track is easy. You need only to apologize and replay the scene with a more appropriate behavior.

- *Beware the S.A.T.s.* As you attempt to change your behavior, it is common to hear a cacophony of sensory-activated tapes ("You can't teach an old dog new tricks!" "I can't do it!" "This feels phony, awkward, like I'm play acting."). Challenge such pointed self-talk with truthful alternatives ("Role playing is the feeling you get before internalizing something new" or "Of course I can do it. I just did!"). If that doesn't work, do what you would do if someone else were giving you such unhelpful advice: thank them for sharing and move on.

We said earlier that we'd need to strive to recognize, appreciate, and learn from our differences. Appreciating a lesson that might feel painful when recognized is another challenge, which brings us to our third axiom.

Axiom Three: Love Conquers All, If Conquering Is Not the Goal

The notion of unconditional positive regard of ourselves and others—of love with no strings attached—is the ideal of human learning and development. The extent to which this ideal fuels our individual journeys is a matter of personal choice. (The ideal, in the words of Saint Francis of Assisi, is "to seek to comfort rather than to be comforted, to understand than to be understood, to love than to be loved.") The axiom, however, has an important practical implication. Remember that a feedback exchange, at least as we have been approaching it, is meant to be a gift giving-and-receiving process. My objective for sharing *appreciates*—specific praise and constructive criticism—has nothing to do with conquering you. Conquering—putting you one down or me one up—and win-win outcomes are different intentions. I am hoping to give you a gift, if you choose to use it, to assist you in improving yourself. Win-win feedback, like love, is intended to build you up, not put you down. (The ways in which we play the putdown game are subtle. Using the word *but* in an *appreciate* statement acts to wipe away the praise ["I like . . . but I dislike . . ."]. In contrast, the word *and* acknowledges the good while building further improvement ["I like . . . and I dislike . . ."].)

To depreciate another person is to behave in a way that lowers the person's estimated value, the person's esteem in his or her own or others' eyes. The antonym (or antidote) for *depreciation* is *appreciation*. However, the antonym for *appreciate* is not simply *depreciate*. The list extends to include "to despise, to look upon with contempt or aversion." In other words, the lack of appreciation for our differences will result in an aversion to or contempt for them, which is not fertile ground for any relationship.

We all need to feel loved, to receive feedback that tells us we are appreciated for who we are and for the better human beings we are struggling to become. In that need we are all very similar. Where we are quite different is in what it takes to make us feel appreciated. In this regard, our tip is quite straightforward. Complimenting each other more often—appreciating our individual uniqueness and strengths—will set the stage for learning how to be better able to use our differences to complement each other. Mutual respect will lead to cooperation, itself a force leading to mutual respect.

Satisfying this human need to feel loved is uniquely challenging. In the absence of an effective feedback process, the love and appreciation we offer as givers will most often mirror the kind of love and appreciation we ourselves would feel most comfortable accepting as receivers; thus the familiar prescription that we should "do unto others as we would have them do unto us."

The examples we've just explored and our experience suggest an updated prescription and our last axiom.

Axiom Four: "Do Unto Others As *They* Would Have You Do Unto Them"

Yes, you read that correctly. How do I find out what you would have me do unto you? What can I do when I sincerely want to help you meet your needs? What can I do when I sincerely want to show you how much I appreciate you? The answer is the same: I become both a skilled giver and a skilled receiver. I must become party to a continuous dynamic exchange process aimed at increasing both my awareness of my behavior and its consequences, my ABCs.

A. I increase my *awareness*. I ask you what you need, what will make you feel appreciated.

B. I try my best to deliver the *behavior* you've asked for.

C. I monitor the *consequences*, and I ask you for feedback as to how I'm doing.

This three-step process, while it sounds simple enough, is not necessarily easy to implement. Minding our ABCs will provide the feedback that the specifics of *how* we need to behave toward one another are not always the same. However, despite these differences in how, *what* we all need is remarkably similar—to be understood and accepted for the miracles we really are.

10

· ·

The Truth of the Consequences

It comes to a moral issue (stamina, strength of courage) whether one applies what one has learned into the real world.

—Carl Jung, Collected Works

In Chapter One, we the authors sought to provide readers with a handle on the "consummate skill and delicacy" needed to uproot and reframe the detrimental assumptions and fears we all carry about giving and receiving direct feedback. This process is the life blood of our very existence, and a process this vital should not be allowed to put fear into people's hearts. All of us need to improve our ability to give and receive direct feedback by following in the footsteps of champions in other walks of life.

As the learning points of the previous chapters unfolded, it is likely that you found yourself nodding your head and saying, "That makes common sense." The steps to becoming a champion are commonly known. A listing of some prescriptive steps that relate to our life's journey could sound like this:

- I need to become self-aware. I need to know how I am behaving now.

- To achieve this level of self-awareness, to be able to line up and compare my intention with my impact,

I need a second—and perhaps even a third—opinion from people willing to tell me honestly how I'm coming across to them.

- I need to try to be as honest and compassionate when asked to be a giver as I would want others to be when I am a receiver.

- I need to develop the flexibility and skill to allow me to effectively exhibit the wide range of behaviors diverse individuals—each with unique needs—will require of me, as I will require of them.

- I need constant updates so I can monitor the consequences of my behavior and self-correct my actions as needed.

While the words you've read in the previous pages may make common sense, they do not, as we know, always become common practice. Let's review for a moment where the gap between common sense and common practice, the challenge of our imperfect natures, has taken us. In Chapter One we began with a glimpse into the deliberations of the U.S. Supreme Court and of the courts of Colorado and Texas. Then we jumped across the ocean to Bambi's residence in the woods outside of Vienna. In Chapter Four we saw that sixty-second interchanges around the kitchen stove could leave sour tastes not unlike those caused by equally quick "by-the-way" and "hit-and-run" interchanges in our corporate hallways. In Chapter Six we realized that, if another person spoke to us the way our S.A.T.s do regularly, we'd turn those people off. In Chapter Seven we visited treatment rooms where patients put pillow cases over their heads and found dynamics paralleling those in the highest government chambers. Also in Chapter Seven we considered the painful truth that all of us, like the emperor, are trying to cover ourselves with nonexistent clothes. We had to examine honestly our truthfulness to our leaders and to ourselves.

Such a far-reaching journey! All these stops along our brief tour involve human beings interacting, doing the best they can. And the Supreme Court opinion in the Charlotte Horowitz case reminded us that, as Goodman (1979, pp. 86–87) says, "everyone's self-image is formed in some measure by the way they are seen, and the way they see themselves being seen. . . . It happens all the time." As a consequence, every encounter with another human being is an opportunity to enhance, modify, and incorporate into ourselves another's vision of how we are seen. Interpersonal feedback is an ongoing process, and its consequences are so ubiquitous and essential to the functioning of our lives, that we take it for granted—until it fails us.

Cause and Effect

We have free choice. Sometimes the choices we make cause ourselves and others harm—mental, physical, legal, emotional, and spiritual. The first time this happens we can justifiably pass it off as an accident, an honest mistake. But what do we call it when we apologize, promise not to do it again, and then persist in the same behavior while professing to expect different consequences? In truth, there are two phrases that capture this behavioral dynamic: acting stupid and acting crazy. Labeling our own behavior this way is not meant to be harsh or laden with judgment but merely to describe a possible truth about our human natures. We are also very capable of behaving in addictive, compulsive, codependent ways. However—although it is not easy, by any means—we also have the capacity to change our behavior toward others and our image of ourselves.

Our self-image impacts our behavior. Everything we say to another person and everything we say to ourselves carries a consequence. Feedback will confirm whether the consequence is what we expect. If we are unhappy with the consequences, we can alter our behavior. If we keep doing what we've been doing, we keep getting what we've gotten.

Others are affected by our words, music, and dance. Their reaction—the words, music, and dance they perform in kind—returns some part of our actions right back to us, which, in turn, influences how we react to their reactions. And the beat goes on. We can act to keep each other upbeat or to keep beating each other up. We can learn to keep in step together or keep stepping on one another's toes. We can choose words that jeopardize or harmonize. It takes a mutually concerted effort to act in concert.

The only guarantee that we get as a gift of being born is the freedom to choose, and the price tag it carries is the responsibility for the consequences of our choices. Although the freedom to choose is universal, some of us find this freedom easier to actualize than others. This theory of interpersonal relativity is what makes the world go round. Whether or not "what comes around" has the quality of being the win-win we've offered is very much a function of the quality of "what goes around." Both are totally dependent upon the interpersonal and, as Jung reminded us, the moral quality of the feedback we give and receive.

Avoiding the Cataclysm

In this closing section, to honor our opening premise that a guide on feedback would be woefully incomplete if it did not resonate with our spiritual cores, we the authors are going to make a few personal statements about the lose-lose implications of not refining our win-win feedback skills. We invite you to join us as we step outside of our self-limiting habitual thinking.

First, let's consider the global situation we have allowed ourselves to get into. As a society, we continue to make choices that invite direct harm to ourselves and others, despite the feedback screaming at us that our actions must change. We are afraid to walk in our polluted, violent cities at night, and millions of us fear our emotionally polluted homes. Johnny can't read. Jill doesn't have a home. Jack's hooked on drugs. Our U.S. government spends $60 on the technology of destruction for every $1 spent on education. Visions of the bleakness of human relations around the globe vary only by degree. To alter these frightening truths, we must be prepared to get back to basics, to begin with the truth of how we got ourselves into this mess in the first place.

At the most fundamental level, individuals are the basic building blocks of every social system, from families to businesses to cities to states to nations. In the business we call living, our interpersonal communications serve as a global net that encompasses the five billion of us.

Like a very complicated chemical compound, several trillion individual interpersonal relationship pairs stretch out to become our global community. When feedback is working well between any two people, do we not often speak of there being "good chemistry"? When the process fails any one of us, several of us might feel the consequences. Smart employees will steer clear of a boss who has just been chewed out by another boss. Similarly, when two parents are continuously at each other's throats, the children—and then their children—are adversely affected. The mistakes of one generation affect the next generation, and the mess snowballs. Like many phenomena in nature, the consequences of poorly managed relationships can grow exponentially.

The end results, the bottom-line consequences of this theory of interpersonal relativity, are justifiably frightening, and they couldn't be more cataclysmic. Win-lose as a viable global outcome is a myth. We either learn together to play the game of life in a win-win fashion or together we experience the lose-lose consequences.

In our opening chapter, we the authors said we hoped to empower each other to be a party to the greatest gift we all could give to and receive from one another. This gift, we ventured to suggest, was the ability to see ourselves as others see us.

We are confident that by giving and receiving gifts of this nature—these glimpses into our evolving human natures—we will realize what special persons—as unique as falling snowflakes—we really are.

Your Feedback on Ours

Dear Reader,

Every relationship experiences its share of what we've called pregnant moments. We feel as if we're groping to find just the right thing to say; yet, sometimes in ways that we seem hard-pressed to explain, the perfect words, music, and dance seem to emerge. A small transformation occurs right before our very eyes: a win-win relationship takes yet another step forward.

We believe those pregnant moments are worth their weight in gold, not just to the parties who felt their almost spiritual power. Since progress—not perfection—is our lot in life, such moments can also serve as learning opportunities for all of us. So we have two *asks* of you in the way of feedback.

1.   Your Own D.A.P.
We would be very appreciative if you would take a moment and

- *Describe* what reading the book meant to you personally

- *Appreciate,* in detail, the pros and cons you experienced

- *Prescribe* what you'd like to see more, less, or the same of in the future.

You can fax us your D.A.P. to 808–528–2434 or e-mail it to [temenos@lava.net].

2.   Your Own Inspiring Pregnant Moment
We would love to collect a series of win-win feedback vignettes; stories about real people struggling to provide one another the gift of realizing what special persons we all are. If you'd be willing to be interviewed by one of the authors as to the general circumstances surrounding one of your own win-win feedback pregnant moments, please use the fax or e-mail numbers just listed to let us know. We will *anonymously* summarize, categorize, and analyze these rare learning opportunities and find a way to feed them back to all of us.

If you would like any more information about any of Temenos® ABCs programs or The Behavior Minder® resources referred to in this book, just give us an *ask* at the same fax or e-mail numbers.

We certainly hope this book has sharpened your awareness of and sensitivity to the oceans of feedback that we swim in continuously.

Appendix

· ·

A Sample Behavior Minder®

WEDNESDAY, 14 AUGUST 1996

Dear ABCs Colleague,

Welcome to a growing body of people committed to increasing their awareness of their behavior and its consequences, the keys of the ABCs of win-win relationships. The Behavior Minder® has been designed to enable you to get "a 360-degree feedback snapshot 365 days a year." Its foundation rests upon three core values:

1. We are each 100 percent accountable for our 50 percent of the quality of any relationship.

2. Unsigned anonymous feedback does not contribute to the trust essential to all win-win relationships.

3. Progress—not perfection—is our lot in life (which is why feedback is the "breakfast of champions").

The eight distinct *styles* and forty-eight clear specific behaviors on which you will receive feedback

- Are based on the day-to-day win-win experiences of thousands of people just like yourself

- Are easy to interpret and translate into action

- Will enable you to compare and contrast your awareness of your own behavior with the consequences as experienced by the other person
- And, like all tools, depend upon your interpersonal skills and heartfelt intentions for successful application

Feedback is available to you in three separate but related forms:

1. One Page Executive Summary

For each individual observer from whom you have requested feedback, a one-page executive summary will provide a sample of the many current behavioral strengths that characterize the relationship and specifically which behaviors your observer would like you to do more of and/or less of in the future to strengthen the win-win quality of your relationship.

2. Extensive Individual Analysis

For each individual observer from whom you have requested feedback, you will also receive an extensive report of the details behind the One Page Executive Summary. We encourage you to use the breadth and depth of rich insights this level of analysis can provide.

3. Extensive Summary Analysis

Each of your many relationships is—and should be—treated as unique. However, tremendous advantages can be made in our awareness of our behavior and its consequences from studying patterns we exhibit across our many unique relationships. Such information can be invaluable in helping us to identify behavioral blind spots and habitual patterns that prevent us from enjoying the benefits of more extensive win-win relationships.

Finally, The Behavior Minder® was designed with one overriding objective in mind, best captured by the following quote:

If I could give you one thing, I would give you the ability to see yourself as others see you. Then you would realize what a truly special person you are. —Anonymous

The Behavior Minder® Executive Summary

Bill R. Schult, on August 14, 1996, you requested John A. Doe to share his perceptions of how often you use each of the forty-eight behaviors at the core of all win-win relationships and which five specific behaviors he would like you to consider doing more or less of to further strengthen the win-win quality of your relationship.

These behaviors fall into two broad categories reflecting our use of push and pull energy. We push energy when our primary objective is to have our thoughts and feelings better understood by another person. Similarly, we use pull energy when our primary objective is to better understand another person's thoughts and feelings. In a win-win relationship, both parties understand and feel understood.

The following chart provides a picture of the percentage agreement you and he reported with respect to the frequency with which you exhibited each of the forty-eight behaviors. "Right On" means perfect agreement; "Close Enough" means you were within one scale point of one another; and "Missed Target" means the difference was two or more scale points. (These "misses" can be the gateway to identifying the normal human blind spots you and John are struggling with in your relationship, unknowingly.)

A sample of the many specific behaviors that reflect relationship strengths—behaviors where you were "right on"—in terms of you both perceiving your use of that behavior, follows directly after the chart. Finally, the specific behaviors—The Keys to a Stronger Relationship—John would like you to consider changing in frequency are listed.

We encourage you to use this report and the detailed results provided in the Extensive Individual Analysis report to develop an action plan to further strengthen your relationship with John.

A sample of the behaviors where you both agree on the extent to which they are used is as follows.

Percentage Agreement Graph

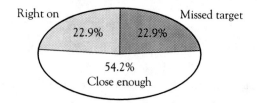

1. Give the time and attention John needs to get points across.

2. Communicate your understanding of how a situation makes John feel.

3. Use well-reasoned arguments to support proposals.

4. Stress the importance of pulling together to achieve common goals.

5. Gracefully accept feedback.

6. Face up to important issues.

7. Apologize for mistakes.

8. Ask directly about the effects your behavior has on John.

The Keys to a Stronger Relationship

The specific behaviors John would like to see you exhibit more or less are

Action	Behavior
More	Express appreciation when John does something well.
More	Describe possibilities in ways that encourage John to share enthusiasm and commitment.
More	Offer suggestions that build on John's ideas.
More	Tell John what you don't like about what he is doing.
More	Give your support when John is facing difficult situations.

Extensive Individual Analysis

Bill, in your Executive Summary you received the headlines of your ABCs with John A. Doe. The information that follows is intended to add richness and depth to the insights you have already about the quality of this win-win relationship.

This report will be divided into three sections:

1. *Push* and *Pull* Energy Styles

2. Digging Deeper: Unmasking the Picture Behind the Styles Scores

3. Specific Changes to Consider

Each section begins with a brief informational input to help you understand the feedback data that follows. A "call to action" concludes the report.

1. *Push* and *Pull* Energy Styles

The Two Energy Modes

Reference was made in your Executive Summary of the use of two distinct types of energy we use in all of our human interactions. In all of our relationships, we are either using our energy to *push* our thoughts, feelings, or ideas toward someone or striving to *pull* thoughts, feelings, or ideas from someone.

Over the long term we will use both—to varying degrees—but at any given moment, we can only be using one of these forms of energy. If two people try to use exactly the same mode of energy at exactly the same instant, it can cause a problem in the relationship. An interruption for example, occurs when one person interjects his own *push* energy while the other person is still *push*ing hers! Just as we've all experienced with a swinging door, over time relationships require a balance of *push* and *pull* energies to work smoothly.

A simple index provides a clear idea of your own relative use of *push* and *pull* energies and the ways your perception compares with John's:

My *Push* Energy Index = 52 percent   **John's View = 46 percent**
My *Pull* Energy Index = 48 percent   **John's View = 54 percent**

Your total *push* and *pull* energy indexes therefore total 100 percent. Please keep in mind as you look at these indexes that there are no right or wrong scores. You and John are the only judges of what a balanced relationship needs to look like—from an energy point of view—between the two of you.

The following charts compare your use of *push* and *pull* energy as perceived by both yourself and John:

The Eight Behavior Styles

Each of the *push* and *pull* energy modes previously described is made up of four specific styles.

Push Styles When you *push* you can *describe* what has happened or is happening, *prescribe* what should or must happen in the future, *appreciate* the significance of what has happened or is happening, and *inspire* others to work with you in the future to achieve common goals.

Describe and *prescribe* are factually based styles. When you are making rational proposals and suggestions for what will, should, or must happen in the future, you are using *push* energy to *prescribe*. When you are providing or debating facts, data, and reasons, you are using *push* energy to *describe*.

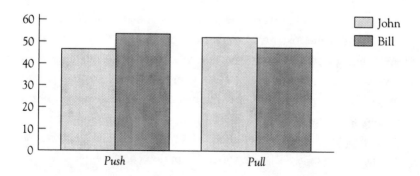

Appreciate and *inspire* are emotionally based styles. When you are providing feedback directly to a person as to how you feel about their past or current behavior or ideas, you are using your *push* energy to *appreciate*. When your feelings are being used to rouse another person to join with you in achieving some future-oriented goal, then you are using *push* energy to *inspire*.

Pull Styles When you pull you can *attend* by making yourself receptive to what the other person is trying to *push*; *ask* questions that will help the other person express their thoughts, feelings, or ideas; use verbal and nonverbal ways to let the other person know you understand their thoughts and ideas; and *empathize* when the other person is expressing emotion.

Attend is almost exclusively exhibited nonverbally. Put another way, people know we are not paying attention when we interrupt them frequently, fumbling with papers while they are talking and the like. People will feel sincerely *pulled* when you ask questions that demonstrate you have an open mind, whether or not you agree. "Leading the witness" by asking questions designed to *pull* a person around to your position (or entrap them) will not be well received.

Demonstrating that you *understand* helps a person to be convinced you are really paying attention to what they are saying and listening to them with an open mind. Just because you *understand* a person, however, does not mean that you agree or disagree; it means that you are explicitly acknowledging that the other person's message has been received. When the message being sent includes how the person is feeling about an issue or about themselves, the most powerful way for you to acknowledge its receipt is to *empathize*.

Push and Pull Style Feedback

Push and *pull* style feedback related to your relationship with John is available in two forms. The bar graph that follows provides a picture of how your own view of the eight styles compares and contrasts with

John's view. (Because each of the eight styles is made up of six specific behavioral items, a style score can range from 0 to 30.)

Careful study of the graph can give you a mental picture of how close and/or far apart you and John might be with respect to your use of each of the eight styles. In addition, you can get an image of how you both see the intensity of the total *push* and *pull* energy being put into the relationship by noticing where on the Y axis an "average" of your style scores might pass.

Intensity, in other words, is like a measure of volume, or how strongly a particular style message is being communicated and/or received. The fact that you and John may disagree on your intensity level for any given style and/or overall does not mean there is anything bad or wrong going on. It may simply mean that one or the other of you now has the opportunity to "recalibrate" yourselves, as a sending or a receiving instrument of win-win communications. (You will gain many potential insights into this dimension of intensity from the Extensive Summary Analysis available to you.)

Finally, the raw data that went into creating the graphs and energy indices you looked at earlier follow after the graphs.

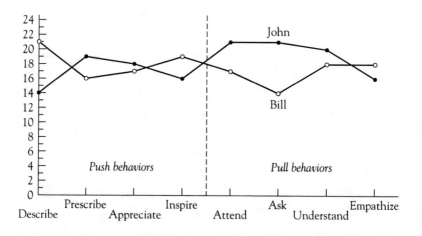

Raw Data

	John	Bill	Rank Difference
Push Behavior Total	67	73	
Pull Behavior Total	78	67	

Push Behaviors			
Describe	14 (4.0)	21 (1.0)	3.0
Prescribe	19 (1.0)	16 (4.0)	3.0
Appreciate	18 (2.0)	17 (3.0)	1.0
Inspire	16 (3.0)	19 (2.0)	1.0

Pull Behaviors			
Attend	21 (1.5)	17 (3.0)	1.5
Ask	21 (1.5)	14 (4.0)	2.5
Understand	20 (3.0)	18 (1.5)	1.5
Empathize	16 (4.0)	18 (1.5)	2.5

So What Does This Mean?

You've already seen what your pattern of energy use is—*push* versus *pull*—from both your own and John's point of view. The frequency with which you use each of the four *push* and *pull* styles is the next important area of concern.

The absolute raw scores that have been plotted on your graphs have also been converted to rank-orders—the numbers in parentheses after each of the style scores. (This will equalize any potential scaling biases that may exist.) This ranking perspective will allow you to see quickly and clearly both your own patterns and the correlation or overlap between your views and John's. Please keep in mind as you review these data that a low ranking does not mean you exhibit that style infrequently. Rather it only means, relative to your use of all the styles, you are not likely to use it as often first off. (It's like cooking. You use a range of spices but not necessarily in the same order or proportions!)

Consequently, if you and John were in perfect agreement on your relative use of *push* or *pull* styles, the absolute difference between your two sets of rankings would be zero. If you were in complete disagreement the absolute difference would be eight.

As a general rule of thumb, we have labeled as "high agreement" any absolute difference of two or less, "low agreement" as any absolute difference of six or more, and "moderate agreement" as anything in between.

Your View Bill, at whatever absolute level of intensity you have chosen to exhibit your *push* energy, in your own mind—in your relationship with John—you are most likely to use *describe*, next most likely to use *inspire*, and least likely to use *prescribe*.

With respect to your use of *pull* styles, you are most likely to use *understand* and *empathize* equally, next most likely to use *attend*, and least likely to use *ask*.

John's View From John's point of view, with respect to the *push* styles, you are most likely to use *prescribe*, next most likely to use *appreciate*, and least likely to use *describe*.

With respect to the *pull* styles, you are most likely to use *attend* and *ask* equally, next most likely to use *understand*, and least likely to use *empathize*.

ABCs Style Correlation With respect to the four *push* styles, you and John are in low agreement as to your frequency of use.

With respect to the four *pull* styles, you and John are in low agreement as to your frequency of use.

2. Digging Deeper: Unmasking the Picture Behind the Style Scores

Each of the eight styles is made up of six specific behavioral items. As a result, total style scores can often mask very important blind spots in your relationships.

Let us examine an example. You and a particular observer might be in perfect alignment that your total use of the *appreciate* style was at a frequency level of 24. Close examination of each of your individual scores on the six items that go into making up this *appreciate* score might reveal the following. You see yourself always (a score of 5) exhibiting item numbers 3 and 19 (dealing with the praise components of *appreciate*) and never (a score of 0) exhibiting item numbers 11 and 27 (dealing with the constructive criticism components of *appreciate*). Your observer might, on the other hand, see the same behaviors exactly opposite to you. She might feel she is always being criticized and never being praised! The total *appreciate* score would mask this vitally important set of blind spots in your relationship.

To unmask any significant differences being hidden behind total style scores, we need to be able to compare—item by item, within a style—what you and John are reporting as the frequency with which you exhibit each of the six specific behaviors that make up a style. (You have already seen in the headlines in the "Right on" versus "Close enough" versus "Missed target" data in your One Page Executive Summary.)

The following pages provide a graphic picture of this comparison. To help you see the possible patterns that may exist in behaviors you are overestimating or underestimating, we have created the Summary of Individual Item Discrepancies table, which follows the last page of charts. The table contains only those items scored as "missed targets" (where you and John disagreed by two or more points in either direction).

Remember: Blind spots in the messages sent and/or received are normal dynamics in all human relationships. As we stated earlier, we are each 100 percent accountable for our 50 percent of the quality of any relationship, and as a consequence of our human natures, progress—not perfection—is our lot in life.

Describe Response Analysis

The numbers along the bottom of the *describe* graph refer to the following behaviors:

01: Clearly explain the basis for decisions.

09: Use well-reasoned arguments to support proposals.

17: Use well-reasoned arguments to support counterproposals.

25: Offer well-reasoned counterarguments when you disagree with John.

33: Openly provide information John might not normally have.

41: Admit mistakes.

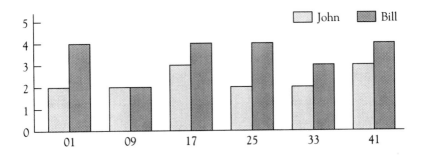

Prescribe Response Analysis

The numbers along the bottom of the *prescribe* graph refer to the following behaviors:

02: Offer suggestions that get right to the point.

10: Tell John clearly what you want.

18: Offer suggestions that build on John's ideas.

26: State your needs and expectations reasonably.

34: Keep John's attention on issues you feel are important.

42: Offer mutually beneficial exchanges and incentives.

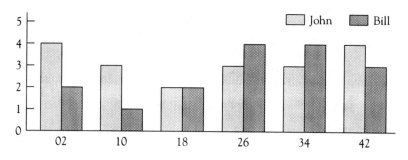

Appreciate Response Analysis

The numbers along the bottom of the *appreciate* graph refer to the following behaviors:

03: Express appreciation when John does something well.

11: Express your dissatisfaction when John doesn't do something well.

19: Tell John what you like about what John is doing.

27: Tell John what you don't like about what John is doing.

35: Gracefully accept feedback.

43: Apologize for mistakes.

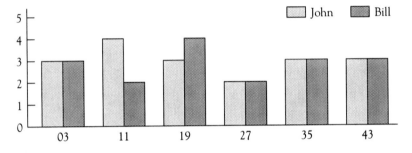

Inspire Response Analysis

The numbers along the bottom of the *inspire* graph refer to the following behaviors:

04: Describe possibilities in ways that encourage John to share enthusiasm and commitment.

12: Use metaphors and vivid descriptions to heighten John's enthusiasm about possibilities.

20: Stress the importance of pulling together to achieve common goals.

28: Emphasize the values that you have in common.

36: Talk from the heart about values and ideals.

44: Encourage John to do more than he thought was possible.

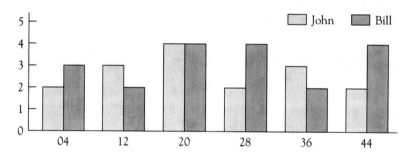

Attend Response Analysis

The numbers along the bottom of the *attend* graph refer to the following behaviors:

05: Give the time and attention John needs to get his point across.

13: Pay careful attention without interrupting when John is trying to make a point.

21: Focus carefully on concerns that John expresses.

29: Back off if the timing is not right.

37: Face up to important issues.

45: Remain patient and receptive when John disagrees with or challenges your point of view.

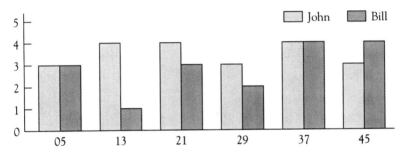

Ask Response Analysis

The numbers along the bottom of the *ask* graph refer to the following behaviors:

06: Ask for the basis of John's decisions.

14: Ask John for suggestions.

22: Ask questions such as, "Could you give me a few examples to help me understand?"

30: Ask questions such as, "How can I help?" or "How can I support you?"

38: Focus on questions such as, "What can we learn from this mistake?" rather than "Who is to blame?"

46: Ask directly about the effects your behavior has on John.

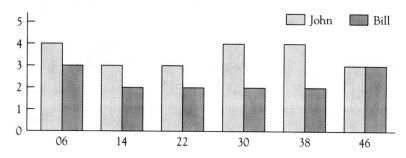

Understand Response Analysis

The numbers along the bottom of the *understand* graph refer to the following behaviors:

07: Communicate your understanding by paraphrasing what John has said.

15: Act as a sounding board to help clarify John's thinking.

23: Summarize areas of agreement or mutual interest.

31: Try to clarify and explore points on which you differ or disagree.

39: Communicate understanding through the tone of the voice.

47: Communicate your understanding in nonverbal ways.

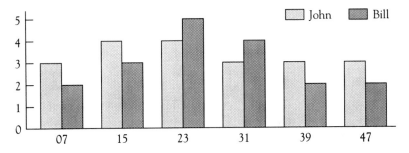

Empathize Response Analysis

The numbers along the bottom of the *empathize* graph refer to the following behaviors:

08: Communicate your understanding of how a situation makes John feel.

16: Help to clarify John's feelings.

24: Show your genuine desire to find out how John feels.

32: Give your support when John is facing difficult situations.

40: Give John the confidence to disclose how he feels about himself.

48: Empathize with John.

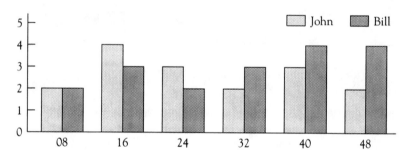

Summary of Individual Item Discrepancies

John Versus Bill

Overall distribution of Percentage Discrepancies

1.	Percentage of items where the discrepancy was zero*	25.0
2.	Percentage of items where the discrepancy was minor*	54.17
3.	Percentage of items where the discrepancy was marked*	20.83

Missed Targets (2 or more points)

Behaviors you have overestimated:

- Clearly explain the basis for the decisions.
- Offer well-reasoned counterarguments when you disagree with John.
- Emphasize the values that you have in common.
- Encourage John to do more than he thought was possible.
- Empathize with John.

Behaviors you have underestimated:

- Offer suggestions that get right to the point.
- Tell John clearly what you want.
- Express your dissatisfaction when John doesn't do something well.
- Pay careful attention without interrupting when John is trying to make a point.

*Remember: Zero means that you and John were in perfect agreement on how frequently you exhibited a specific behavior. Your ABCs—your awareness of your behavior was perfectly in tune with the consequences as experienced by John. Minor means a discrepancy of only one point in either direction. Discrepancies of this magnitude are most often the result of the two people using different scale scores to reflect similar perceptions. Marked means that you and John diverged by two or more points in either direction. Such discrepancies are not normally scaling differences. Rather they can be the gateway to very powerful insights to blind spots you and John struggle with—unknowingly—in your relationship.

- Ask questions such as, "How can I help?" or "How can I support you?"

- Focus on questions such as, "What can we learn from this mistake?" not on "Who is to blame?"

So What Does It Mean?

Since each relationship is unique, the interpretation of these kinds of discrepancies cannot be done in any detail at arm's length. Rather, it is strongly advised that you personally reflect upon and talk with John about any discrepant patterns your data may have uncovered. (See the Behavioral Action Plan at the end of this report.)

There may be opportunities for you both to discover blind spots: areas where you may have been unaware of behaviors you were sending and areas where he may have had his receiver turned off or down and, as a consequence, didn't get your message.

The following questions will be useful in guiding your own reflection and discussions with John.

1. Do your "missed targets" tend to fall into any noticeable patterns of overestimation or underestimation when it comes to

   - *Push* versus *pull* energy modes?
   - Factually oriented (*describe* and *prescribe*) versus emotionally oriented (*appreciate* and *inspire*) *push* styles?
   - *Pull* styles in general?

2. Does your pattern of overestimation versus underestimation give you any insights into the nature of your relationship with respect to John when it comes to any tendencies you sensed existed with respect to

   - Your feeling sometimes like you were overbearing?
   - Your feeling sometimes like you were holding back?
   - Any other particular challenges you knew existed already?

3. What do your own reflections tell you—if anything—about your general feelings about the quality of your relationship with John when it comes to

- How safe it feels to be yourself?
- How much of a sense of win-win equality has existed to date?
- What changes in the relationship might be useful to consider?

3. Specific Changes to *Consider*

We highlight the word *consider* to emphasize a very important point. Since we are each accountable for our half of the quality of any relationship, any request for change—to be successfully met—may well require a *quid pro quo* in return.

For example, in order for you to deliver on someone's request that you *appreciate* more frequently and tell them what it is that you don't like about what they are doing, you may have to request in return that this person *attend* more frequently and pay careful attention without interrupting when you are trying to make your points.

That "it takes two to tango" is just as true in relationships as on the dance floor. Both you and John have to be prepared to accept accountability for the win-win quality of your relationship.

The specific behaviors John has asked you to consider changing are repeated as follows:

Action	Behavior
More	Express appreciation when John does something well.
More	Describe possibilities in ways that encourage John to share enthusiasm and commitment.
More	Offer suggestions that build on John's ideas.
More	Tell John what you don't like about what he is doing.
More	Give your support when John is facing difficult situations.

As you study these specific requests—in spite of the fact that they are from a single individual—you may still see that they do not fall into a random pattern. All or most of them may reflect

- *Push* versus *pull* energy, or vice versa

- One or two specific styles within the *push* or *pull* energy mode

- Five distinct style categories

Regardless of the pattern—if any—which may exist, the behaviors involved in the ABCs are intentionally meant to be very specific so they can more easily be translated into action.

A Call to Action

Many people like yourself have found that transferring their priority change requests to a 3 x 5 card makes it easy to carry around in their pocket. Such immediate awareness of your behavior and its consequences will go a long way toward improving the win-win quality of your relationship with John.

To support you in this effort, we have listed the following sentence stems you can call upon when you are striving to exhibit any of the seven verbal ABCs styles. (*Attend*, the eighth style, is nonverbal and requires only that you "stop, look and listen.")

Finally, we would like to encourage you to have a face-to-face conversation with John. The final pages of this report contain a Behavioral Action Plan. A careful review of this document will enable you to prepare for and implement this conversation in a way that further strengthens the win-win quality of your relationships.

Good luck on this most exciting and important of journeys.

Push		Pull	
Describe		*Attend*	
Prove/Disprove	Because of …	Pay Attention	Stop
Reason/Explain	The facts are …	Tune In	Look
Debate/Argue	The reasons were …	Remain Patient	Listen
Prescribe		*Ask*	
Suggest/Propose	I suggest …	Seek information	Could you expand upon …
Direct/Tell	I need …	Seek suggestions	What would you suggest …
Exchange/Negotiate	I will … if you will	Seek feedback	How can I …
Appreciate		*Understand*	
Give feedback	I (liked or disliked) …	Paraphrase/Reflect	In other words …
Praise/Criticize	I apologize for …	Check understanding	What you're telling me is …
Accept feedback	Thank you.	Summarize/Explore	So you're saying …
Inspire		*Empathize*	
Appeal/Excite	Together we can …!	Track implications	My impression is …
Induce/Evoke	Imagine …!	Communicate	I sense that you're feeling …

Behavioral Action Plan

Bill, this Behavioral Action Plan is designed as a guide for your use in a follow-up conversation with your questionnaire respondents in general. The following criteria might assist you in deciding whether to have a follow-up conversation with John in particular, however it is generally helpful to have a follow-up conversation with all of your questionnaire respondents.

The criteria might include

- The continuing relationship with John is important to you, either professionally, personally or both.

- The health of the relationship has room for improvement, yet is strong enough to have a realistic probability of success.

- There is enough trust in the relationship for both you and John to speak directly and sensitively with each other.

- John is likely to be willing to have a follow-up conversation with you.

- The outcome of this conversation will be of importance and value to you.

Creating the Right Environment

It is important to create the right environment to have this discussion. You may want to consider the following points to increase the possibility that you will get off on the right footing in this conversation.

Selecting a Place

Select a place where you can have a thirty- to-forty-minute discussion

- Without being interrupted or overheard by others.

- At a time when both you and John are not experiencing severe stress.

- When you will have an adequate amount of energy to invest in this conversation.

Identifying Helpful Information

The information you will discuss will have a strong impact on the value of this conversation to you and John. The ABCs questionnaire and John's input on this questionnaire was designed to provide the framework of feedback on your behaviors and behavioral patterns. However, it is not designed to provide all the specifics you may need to change behavior.

Information that may have a positive impact on the relationship and your ability to change are

- Specific examples of behavior John would like to see more or less of

- The types of situations where these behaviors can be exhibited effectively and positively

- A discussion of how your current behavior impacts John

- A discussion of how behavior changes may make John feel

- An assessment of the types of support that would be useful to get from John to help you with these behavior changes

- A discussion of the value of your relationship with John

Beginning the Conversation

The conversation you will have with John must come from you and not a piece of paper. A mechanical lockstep approach may not be of help and, in fact, can backfire on you, even with good intentions.

It is helpful to speak from both your heart and head with John about the information he has provided and the additional information you may need. It is helpful to give some thought to how you may want to start this conversation so you get off on the right footing.

The following guideline is designed for you to complete before you begin your conversation with John. It is designed to give you an opportunity to explicitly use all of the *push* and *pull* styles.

- What specific information would you hope to obtain as a result of this conversation?

- How do you want John to think/feel about you as a result of this conversation?

- What type of positive *appreciate* behavior can you exhibit to John at the beginning of the conversation?

- How might you *empathize* with John?

- What words would you use to *prescribe* to John what you hope to achieve in this conversation?

- How might you *inspire* John?

- Summarize your *understanding* of the high-priority behavior changes John has requested of you.

- What areas would you *ask* for more clarification, examples, and so on?

- What areas may you need to *ask* for help from John?

After your conversation with John, it would be helpful to review the results of your conversation and contrast the results with the plan you just developed. The postconversation conversation is easy to forget, yet at times is where you learn the most.

References

Ash, R., and Higton, B. *Fairy Tales from Hans Christian Andersen.* San Francisco: Chronicle Books, 1992.

Ash, S. "The Pressure to Conform." In Kolb, D., Osland, J., and Rubin, I. (eds.), *Organizational Behavior: An Experiential Approach*, Sixth Edition. Upper Saddle River, N.J.: Prentice Hall, 1995.

Autry, J. A. *Love and Profit: The Art of Caring Leadership.* New York: Morrow, 1991.

Autry, J. A. *Life and Work: A Manager's Search For Meaning.* New York: Aaron Books, 1994.

Blanchard, K., and Johnson, S. *The One-Minute Manager.* New York: Morrow, 1982.

Deng Ming-Dao. (ed.). *365 Tao Daily Meditations.* San Francisco: Harper San Francisco, 1992.

Goodman, E. *Close to Home.* New York: Simon & Schuster, 1979.

Gray, J. *Men Are from Mars, Women Are from Venus.* New York: HarperCollins, 1992.

Hooper, J., and Teresi, D. *The 3-Pound Universe.* New York: Dell, 1986.

Imagine. Cambridge, Mass.: Synectics, 1995.

Janus, I. L. "Managerial Problem Solving." In Kolb, D., Osland, J., and Rubin, I. (eds.), *Organizational Behavior: An Experiential Approach*, Sixth Edition. Upper Saddle River, N.J.: Prentice Hall, 1995.

Jung, C. G. *Bollinger Series: The Collected Works of C. G. Jung* (W. McGuire, executive ed.), Vol. 8: *The Structure and Dynamics of the Psyche* (H. Reed, M. Fordham, and G. Adler, eds.). Princeton, N.J.: Princeton University Press, 1960.

Kolb, D., Osland, J., and Rubin, I. (eds.). *Organizational Behavior: An Experiential Approach*, Sixth Edition. Upper Saddle River, N.J.: Prentice Hall, 1995.

Lancaster, H. "Performance Appraisals Are More Valuable When More Join In." *Wall Street Journal*, July 9, 1996, p. 1.

Levinson, W., and others. "Physician-Patient Communication: The Relationship with Malpractice Claims Among Primary Care Physicians." *Journal of the American Medical Association*, 1997, *277* (7), 553–559.

McGregor, D. "An Uneasy Look at Performance Appraisal." *Harvard Business Review*, 1972, *50* (5), 134.

Milgram, S. "Studies in Social Obedience." In Kolb, D., Osland, J., and Rubin, I. (eds.), *Organizational Behavior: An Experiential Approach*, Sixth Edition. Upper Saddle River, N.J.: Prentice Hall, 1995.

Nezhat, C. "Toxic Emotions: The Clinical Data." In Golemon, D. (ed.), *Emotional Intelligence*. New York: Bantam Books, 1995.

Roberts, E., and Amidom, E. (eds.). *Earth Prayers from Around the World*. San Francisco: Harper San Francisco, 1991.

Rubin, I. "CEOs: Key Holders to World Peace." Honolulu, Hawaii: Temenos, 1991.

Rubin, I. "Total Quality Management: Care Dealers vs. Car Dealers." *Physician Executive Journal of Management*, Sept./Oct. 1992.

Rubin, I., and Fernandez, C. R. *My Pulse Is Not What It Used to Be: The Leadership Challenges in Health Care*. Honolulu, Hawaii: Temenos, 1991.

Rubin, I., and Inguagiato, R. "Behavioral Quality Assurance: A Transforming Experience." *Physician Executive Journal of Management*, Sept./Oct. 1990.

Salten, F. *Bambi: A Life in the Woods*. New York: Simon & Schuster, 1928.

Schutte, J. E. "An Impaired Doctor Cost His Colleagues $5 Million." *Medical Economics*, June 4, 1990, pp. 45–50.

Touchstones: A Book of Daily Meditations for Men. New York: HarperCollins, 1987.

Index

Printed in the United States
102104LV00002B/94-126/A